DISPLAY CABINETS
You Can Customize

DISPLAY CABINETS
You Can Customize

JEFF GREEF

BETTERWAY BOOKS

Cincinnati, Ohio

Disclaimer

To prevent accidents, keep safety in mind while you work. Use the safety guards installed on power equipment; they are for your protection. When working on power equipment, keep fingers away from saw blades, wear safety goggles to prevent injuries from flying wood chips and sawdust, wear headphones to protect your hearing, and consider installing a dust vacuum to reduce the amount of airborne dust in your woodshop. Don't wear loose clothing, such as neckties or shirt with loose sleeves, or jewelry, such as rings, necklaces or bracelets, when working on power equipment, and tie back long hair to prevent it from getting caught in your equipment. The author and editors who compiled this book have tried to make all the contents as accurate as possible. Plans, illustrations, photographs and text have been carefully checked. All instructions, plans and projects should be carefully read, studied and understood before beginning construction. Due to the variability of local conditions, construction materials, skill levels, etc., neither the author nor Betterway Books assumes any responsibility for any accidents, injuries, damages or other losses incurred resulting from the material presented in this book.

A Word About Dimensions

The author and editors who compiled the information for this book have gone over all of the dimensions, drawings, photographs, text and captions to ensure that the information here is accurate. The best woodworkers plan projects through before they cut the first piece of wood. Please take the time to go over all of the dimensions for your project whether you are designing your own or building a project straight out of the book. This practice will not only ensure that you do not waste any wood, but will give you a unique understanding and appreciation of the furniture you are about to build.

Display Cabinets You Can Customize. Copyright © 1995 by Jeff Greef. Printed and bound in the United States of America. All rights reserved. No part of this book may be reproduced in any form or by any electronic or mechanical means including information storage and retrieval systems without permission in writing from the publisher, except by a reviewer, who may quote brief passages in a review. Published by Betterway Books, an imprint of F&W Publications, Inc., 1507 Dana Avenue, Cincinnati, Ohio 45207. 1-800-289-0963. First edition. 2nd printing.

99 98 97 96 95   5 4 3 2

Library of Congress Cataloging in Publication Data
Greef, Jeff
    Display cabinets you can customize / by Jeff Greef.—1st ed.
    p. cm.
    Includes index.
    ISBN 1-55870-389-6
    1. Cabinetwork. 2. Furniture making. 3. Glazing. I. Title.
TT197.G69 1995
684.1'6—dc20   94-47820
                                                      CIP

Edited by R. Adam Blake
Interior design by Brian Roeth
Cover design by Sandy Conopeotis Kent

Betterway Books are available at special discounts for sales promotions, premiums and fund-raising use. Special editions or book excerpts can also be created to specification. For details contact:
    Special Sales Manager
    Betterway Books
    1507 Dana Avenue
    Cincinnati, Ohio 45207

METRIC CONVERSION CHART		
TO CONVERT	**TO**	**MULTIPLY BY**
Inches	Centimeters	2.54
Centimeters	Inches	0.4
Feet	Centimeters	30.5
Centimeters	Feet	0.03
Yards	Meters	0.9
Meters	Yards	1.1
Sq. Inches	Sq. Centimeters	6.45
Sq. Centimeters	Sq. Inches	0.16
Sq. Feet	Sq. Meters	0.09
Sq. Meters	Sq. Feet	10.8
Sq. Yards	Sq. Meters	0.8
Sq. Meters	Sq. Yards	1.2
Pounds	Kilograms	0.45
Kilograms	Pounds	2.2
Ounces	Grams	28.4
Grams	Ounces	0.04

Jeffrey Strong Greef received a B.A. in Classical Literature from the University of California, Santa Cruz, in 1981. From 1984 to 1989 he made sash and door at the Davenport Mill near Santa Cruz, making furniture in his spare time. Combining words and wood, he began to write for magazines such as *Fine Woodworking, Home Mechanix, Workbench, Popular Woodworking, Woodshop News* and others. He edited *Woodwork* magazine in 1989 and 1990, and since then has written on a strictly freelance basis. He presently lives in Santa Cruz, where he is also a disc jockey at KUSP Radio, hosting a program of international folk music.

Part One: Projects

Here are designs, dimensions and construction steps for you to build the display table, display case or curio cabinet of your choice.

CHAPTER ONE

CHAPTER TWO

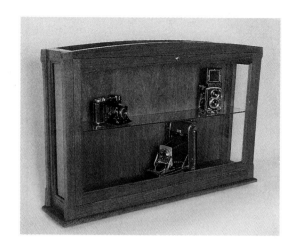

CHAPTER THREE

CURIO CABINETS................................55

Part Two: Techniques

Here are techniques and variations for you to build glazed cabinetry.

Designing and Building Display Tables, Cases and Cabinets

How to Use This Book

In this book you will find dimensioned drawings and step-by-step instruction to build a variety of display tables, cases and cabinets. The purpose of this book is to help you design and build furniture to suit your own personal taste and style. In part one you will find the drawings and instructions to build the projects. In part two you will find variations to help you customize your project.

Glazing

Building display cabinets entails one of the finer aspects of woodworking—glazing techniques. *Glazing* is installing glass into a frame. While this is a challenging technique, it doesn't have to be a difficult one. There are degrees of complexity and difficulty with the joinery required to put glass in wooden frames. Depending on your own skill level and woodworking know-how, you can design the joinery and construction of these projects around your abilities. Here you will find a range of techniques to customize these plans to fit your particular needs. In the first part of the book you will find complete instructions for making three different glazed cabinets, and variations on the three. These variations give you an unlimited choice of how you want to design and build your particular piece. The joinery techniques contained here are the least difficult and complex I could use while still designing a structurally sound cabinet. The techniques sec-

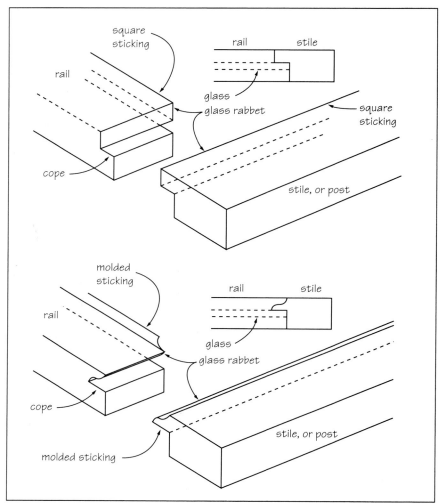

Glazed frame components must have a rabbet into which the glass is placed. The challenge is to join the rabbeted frame components at the corners.

tion contains instructions for more challenging ways of doing frame joinery for glazing, as well as more detailed explanations of jigs and other techniques and materials necessary to do the work.

Glass must be put into a rabbet—rather than a groove like a wood panel—so that it can be replaced if it

breaks. A rabbet is easy to make, but how do you join two rabbeted pieces at a corner joint so that all the surfaces connect tightly? This is the basic problem of glazed frame joinery, and there are numerous solutions.

First let's look at a little terminology for glazed frames. The vertical components are called *posts* when they are integral with the cabinet, and *stiles* when they are on doors. Between the posts or stiles are the *rails*, which butt up against the inside edges of the posts and stiles. Along the inside of the frame is a rabbet that faces toward the middle of the cabinet; the *sticking* is the inside edge of the frame parts not removed by the rabbet—it's the lip that's left by the rabbet that holds the glass. The sticking faces toward the outside of the cabinet and is highly visible.

Because the sticking is highly visible, woodworkers often want to put a molded profile on it to give the frame an attractive, detailed appearance. But in this case you have to join not only a rabbet, but also a molded profile with no gaps at the frame corners.

Designing Glazed Furniture

The design and techniques used to build the furniture featured here use a square sticking (one that is not molded) because it is the easiest to execute and requires minimal tooling. As you can see from the photographs, this makes a very attractive piece of furniture. However, for those of you that want to use molded profiles on the sticking of your cabinets, the second part of this book will show you how. You will find step-by-step instructions for using applied moldings and for making and installing your own profile moldings using a router, a simple hand tool technique for making mitered sticking and more. What you choose to make is up to you. Whatever you choose, all the instruction you will need is here. One method uses an old hand-tool technique that requires less tooling, the other uses modern "stile-and-rail" router bits to achieve the same end. All these techniques are

Illustrated here is the "cope and stick" method of joining stiles and rails. With either a square or molded sticking, make a cope cut on the rail end which fits snugly over the sticking on the stile edge.

directly applicable to all the cabinet designs presented in the book, as well as the variations suggested.

A curved rail on a cabinet gives the piece a unique look indeed. For that reason I have designed two of the three cabinets here with curved top rails. The joinery procedures for curved rails vary a little from those for 90° joints, and you will find complete instructions for handling curved rails here.

Some cabinet designs call for bars within the glazed frames of the cabi-

net. *Bars* are simply thin dividers between pieces of glass in a door or other cabinet frame. Instructions for making bars are included in the techniques section. Those instructions include separate procedures for making bars with each of the sticking-joinery types presented.

Cope and Stick

A common phrase you'll hear associated with glazed frame joinery is "cope and stick." A *cope* is a cut made on the end of a rail where it butts onto the stile or post edge. The purpose of the cope is to make way for the sticking, or *stick*, on the stile so that the parts fit together. The square sticking method used in this plan involves making a square cope on the rail end for the square sticking to fit over.

There's one rather confusing aspect to this kind of work that I want you to think about early on. Every frame has a rabbet around its inside, which creates two separate width dimensions for you to deal with. The first dimension is the total width of the part, including the sticking. The second is the width of the part minus the sticking, or the width of the part from the outer edge to the rabbet.

When you design a frame, you must be aware of these two dimensions. In certain instances, the length of parts (such as some rails and bars) is determined by measuring between the two rabbets of the parts they fit within. Thus, your part dimensions are sometimes dependent on your rabbet dimensions. Just remember that the total width of a part (including sticking) is not necessarily the dimension you use when totaling part dimensions within a frame.

Tools You Will Need

These projects are designed to use ¾"-thick lumber such as you'll find at hardwood lumber stores. There is no need to run out and buy a lot of expensive woodworking equipment to build the furniture in this book. Your existing shop setup should be fine. Machines you'll need include a table saw and a router table; a band saw is helpful for cutting out the curved top rails, but you can use a scroll or saber saw for that work. You need a band saw for the curved feet on the large cabinet, but if you don't have one you can use straight feet as shown in the design variations.

Making the cabriole legs for the table requires a band saw, but you can buy premade cabriole legs from a manufacturer (an address is listed under sources of supply on page 54). If you do that, and use the square sticking design for the frames on the table, the project becomes fast and easy, and can be done in just a few weekends. Instructions to make your own tapering jig are also included; you could easily make tapered legs on your table saw, giving you an attractive alternative to cabriole or turned legs that will also save time. Whatever you decide, all of the instruction is here to help you create your own customized glazed furniture.

Glass Variations

One other addition that you can include on cabinets of this type is leaded glass. Contact a local stained glass worker and ask them for a quote on making a design. So that the contents of the cabinet are visible, I suggest that you use a lot of clear glass in that design, between figures of flowers, birds and beautiful woodworking tools.

PART ONE

PROJECTS

CHAPTER ONE

DISPLAY TABLES
End Tables, Buffet Tables, Coffee Tables

Your most important decision on this project will be what legs to use. Making cabriole legs is time-consuming but very rewarding, and is explained in chapter nine. You can buy premade cabriole legs like those shown on the table in the photo. This is not too expensive, and an easy route to making an attractive table. Finally, you can make straight or tapered legs, or turned legs if you have a lathe. Make your own tapered legs using the tapering jig and instructions in chapter eight. Whatever legs you choose, the joinery, explained here, remains the same. Use the following step-by-step instructions *after* you have carefully planned the construction of your customized display table.

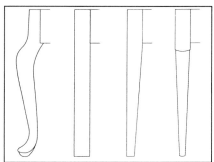

Alternative Leg Designs.

End Tables

Follow the icons at the top of each page to identify part names, dimensions and construction steps for the display table you are making.

END TABLE WITH STRAIGHT LEGS

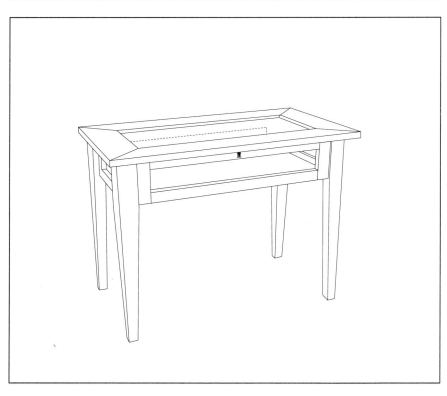

END TABLE WITH TAPERED LEGS

END TABLE WITH TURNED LEGS

END TABLE WITH CABRIOLE LEGS

Coffee Tables

Follow the icons at the top of each page to identify part names, dimensions and construction steps for the display table you are making.

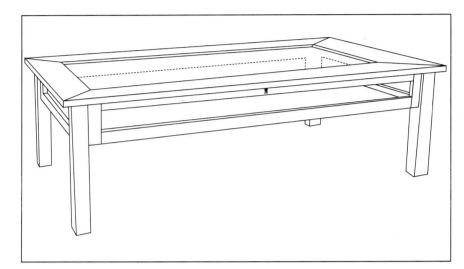

COFFEE TABLE WITH STRAIGHT LEGS

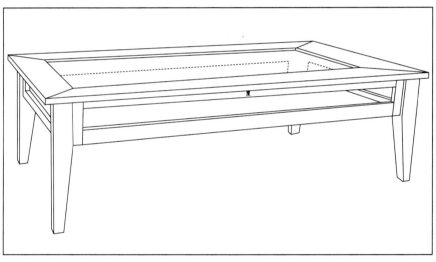

COFFEE TABLE WITH TAPERED LEGS

COFFEE TABLE WITH TURNED LEGS

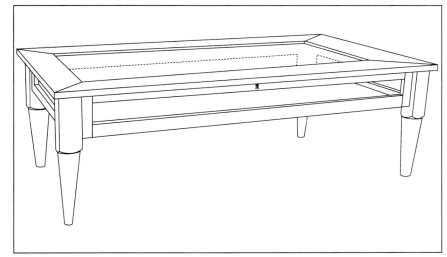

COFFEE TABLE WITH CABRIOLE LEGS

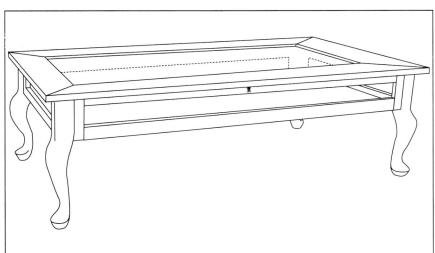

Buffet Tables

Follow the icons at the top of each page to identify part names, dimensions and construction steps for the display table you are making.

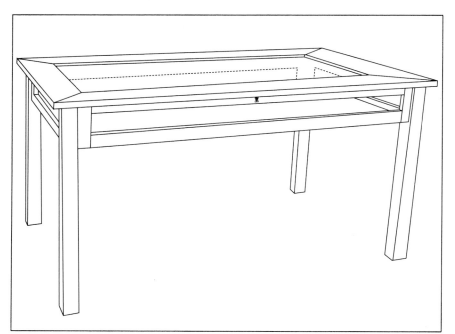

BUFFET TABLE WITH STRAIGHT LEGS

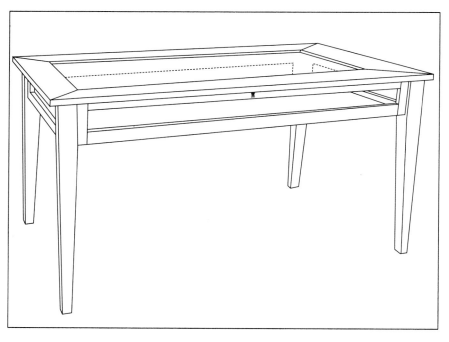

BUFFET TABLE WITH TAPERED LEGS

BUFFET TABLE WITH TURNED LEGS

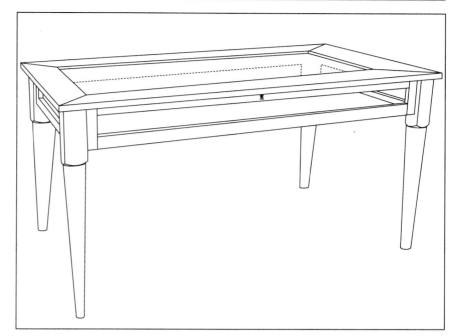

BUFFET TABLE WITH CABRIOLE LEGS

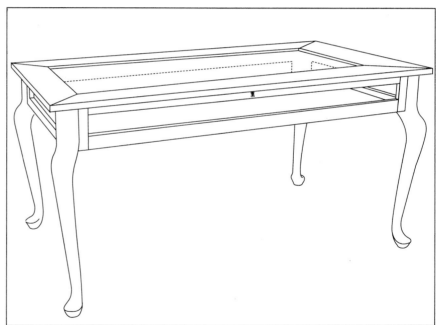

Display Tables
Part Names

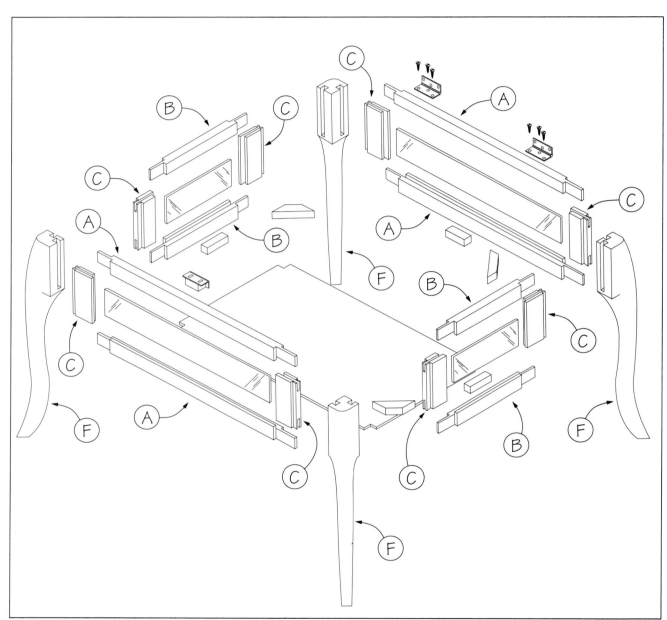

TABLE BASE

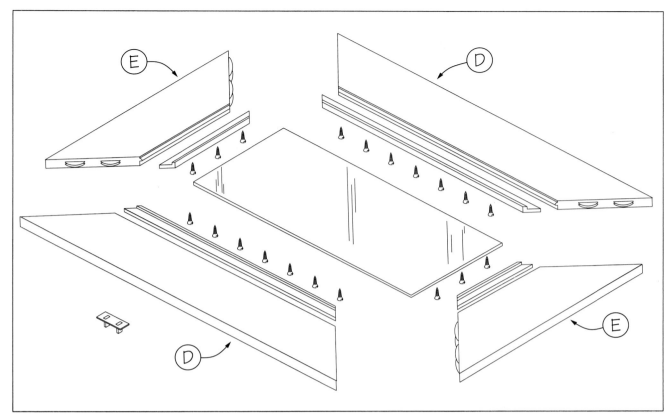

TABLE TOP

PART NAMES—DISPLAY TABLES

(A) rails

(B) rails

(C) posts

(D) top

(E) top

(F) legs

End Table

Dimensions

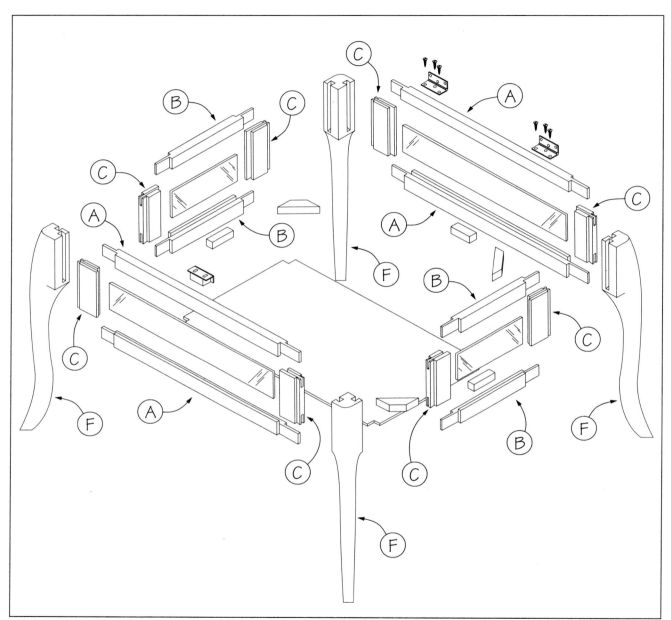

TABLE BASE

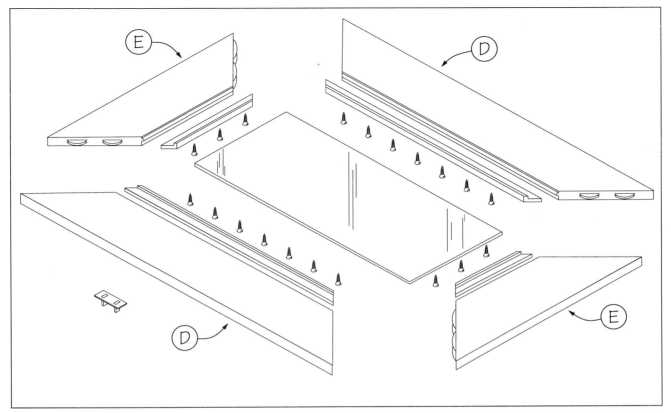

TABLE TOP

CUTTING LIST—END TABLE

¾″ stock:

4-1¼×24	(A) rails
4-1¼×12	(B) rails
8-2×5	(C) posts
2-4×30	(D) top
2-4×18	(E) top
4-2¼×2¼×21	(F) legs (or other dimensions)
1-⅜×14×26	bottom
	plus small pieces for corner blocks, etc.

Coffee Table
Dimensions

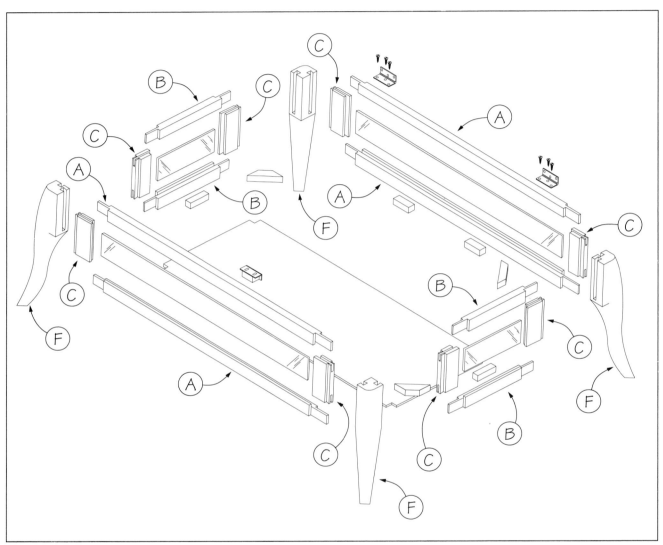

TABLE BASE

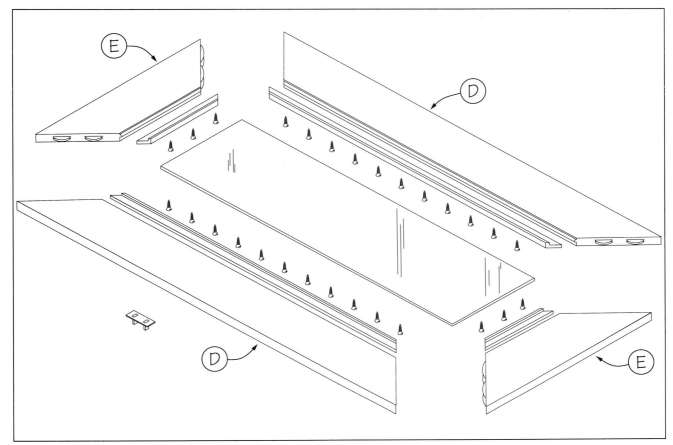

TABLE TOP

CUTTING LIST—COFFEE TABLE

¾″ stock

4-1¼×36	(A) rails
4-1¼×12	(B) rails
8-2×5	(C) posts
2-4×42	(D) top
2-4×18	(E) top
4-2¼×2¼×16	(F) legs (or other dimensions)
1-⅜×14×38	bottom plus small pieces for corner blocks, etc.

Buffet Table

Dimensions

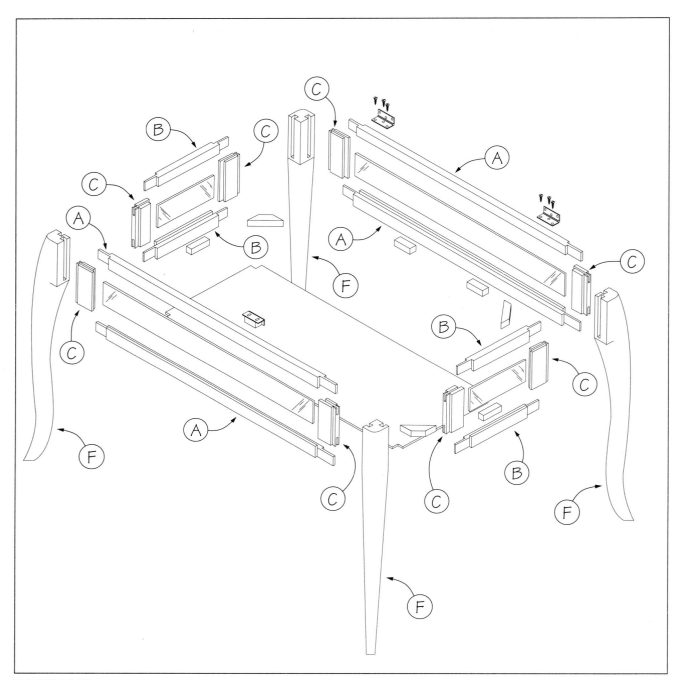

TABLE BASE

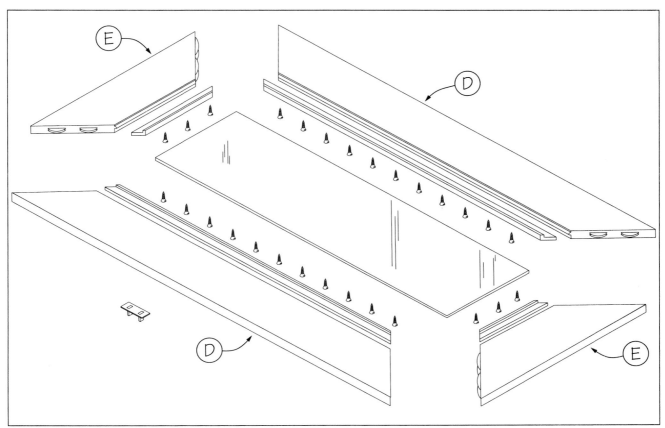

TABLE TOP

CUTTING LIST—BUFFET TABLE

¾″ stock

4-1¼×36	(A) rails
4-1¼×12	(B) rails
8-2×5	(C) posts
2-4×42	(D) top
2-4×18	(E) top
4-2¼×2¼×26	(F) legs (or other dimensions)
1-⅜×14×38	bottom
	plus small pieces for corner blocks, etc.

Display Tables
Construction Steps

STEP 1

Choose the Joinery and Cut out the Parts

Follow the instructions in chapter four for cutting open mortise-and-tenon joints with square sticking to make the four frames that fit between the legs.

STEP 2

Glue the Frames

Glue up the frames from Step 1 as shown at the top right.

STEP 3

Machine the Legs

You will find instructions for making legs in chapter nine. If you make legs, cut the dovetail slots in them before you shape the legs, since a rectangular blank is easier to deal with than a finished leg. If you buy a premade leg, be sure that it is properly supported on the router-table fence while the cuts are made.

STEP 2
Use bar clamps to pull the frames together, but apply minimal pressure so the parts don't bend. Pull the mortises onto the tenons with C-clamps and clamp blocks.

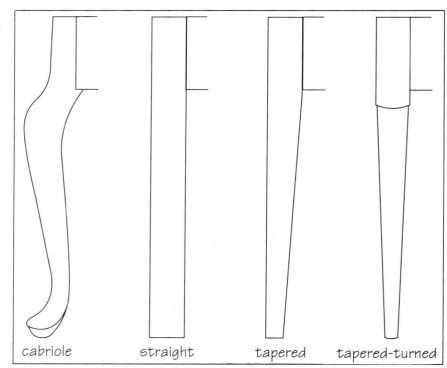

cabriole   straight   tapered   tapered-turned

STEP 3
Alternative Leg Designs. Taper legs on a jointer, band saw or table saw with a tapering jig. Turned legs require a lathe.

STEP 4
Before cutting the dovetail slots, cut clearance slots within the waste with a straight-flute bit. This makes the final dovetail cut easier and safer.

STEP 5
After the clearance slots are cut, leave the fence in the same position and install the dovetail bit. Hold the part firmly against the fence and push into the bit until the part reaches the mark on the table.

STEP 4

Clear out the Waste

The dovetail slots you will make on these legs are fairly deep and large. For that reason it is very important to clear out as much of the waste as you can from the slot before you cut the actual dovetail profile with the dovetail bit. If you don't, the dovetail bit will cut too much wood at once and could stall or throw the work.

Clear the waste with a straight-flute bit as shown at the top left. Use the largest bit you can and still stay within the finished dovetail profile. Set the bit at ¼" high, and set the fence at the correct width from the bit center. (You will need to determine, depending on the width of the leg stock that you use, where the center of the cuts will be.) Make marks on your router table on both sides of the bit. Cut slots on both inside surfaces of each leg as shown by pushing the work along the fence and up to the mark on the table, then retracting. Then raise the bit to ½" and repeat the procedure.

STEP 5

Finish Dovetail Cuts in the Legs

Leave the fence in position and place the dovetail bit in the router. Raise it to ½" above the table and cut slots as shown at the bottom left. When making the cuts from left to right, note that the direction of the bit tends to push the work away from the fence. The waste slot reduces this tendency a great deal, but it's still there, so push the work against the fence hard and move it into the cutter slowly.

Cut Dovetails in the Frames

Cut corresponding dovetails on the ends of the four frames with a vertical fence on the router table as shown at the top right. Make test cuts on scrap of the same thickness to get a dovetail of the correct size, one that fits the slots easily with minimal slop.

STEP 6A
Use a tall vertical fence on the router table to make the sliding dovetails on the ends of the frames. The tall fence is more stable and lets you keep your fingers safely away from the work.

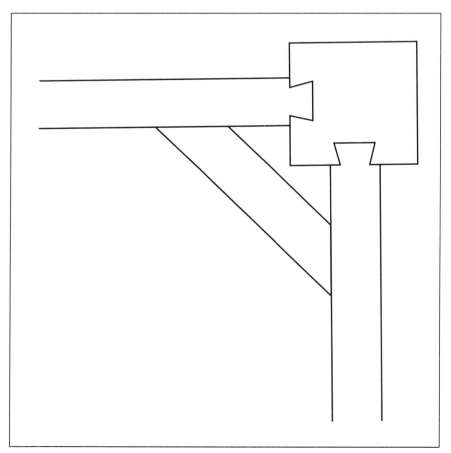

STEP 6B
The exact location of the rails along the leg widths can vary according to how wide a leg you use. Space them so that the dovetails don't overlap.

STEP 7

Notch the ends of the sliding dovetails to fit over the ends of the dovetail slots. Without the notches, the bottom of the slots would be exposed.

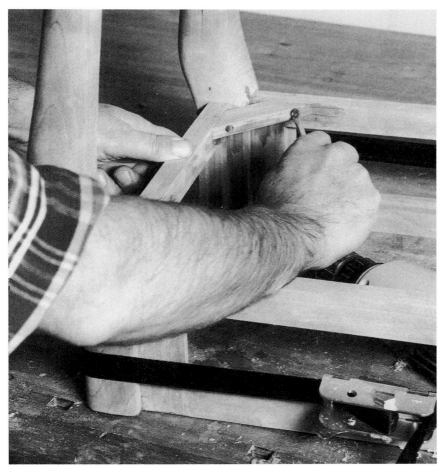

STEP 8

Pull the assembly together with a band clamp or bar clamps, then glue and screw in corner blocks between the frames, as shown.

Cut Notches in Dovetails

Cut notches on the lower ends of the sliding dovetails at ¾" from the bottom of the frames, as shown at the top left.

Attach the Frames to the Legs

Glue the frames to the legs and pull the assembly together with bar clamps or a band clamp as shown at the bottom left. Make ½"-thick corner blocks, then glue and screw them into place in the corners, flush with the bottom as shown.

STEP 9

Attach the Support Blocks

Glue other support blocks at ½" × ½" around the inside bottom perimeters of the frames. Make a bottom by edge-gluing ½"-thick pieces together to achieve the necessary width (which will vary depending upon the legs you use). Or, use a piece of ¼" or ½" hardwood-veneer plywood. Notch the bottom at the corners to fit around the legs. Screw the bottom to the support blocks.

STEP 10

Install Spacers for the Hinges

Glue spacers on the outside top of one of the long rails for hinges. The spacers must hold the hinges beyond the line of the table legs in order for the top to open.

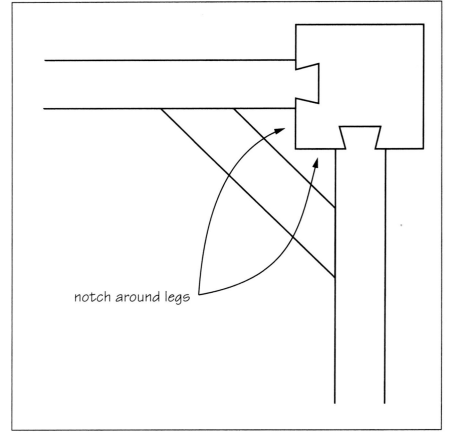

notch around legs

STEP 9

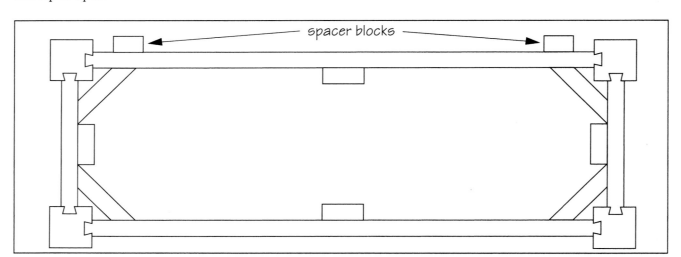

spacer blocks

STEP 10

Glue spacer blocks onto one long rail for the hinges. These spacers hold the hinges far enough away from the legs for the top to clear them as it opens.

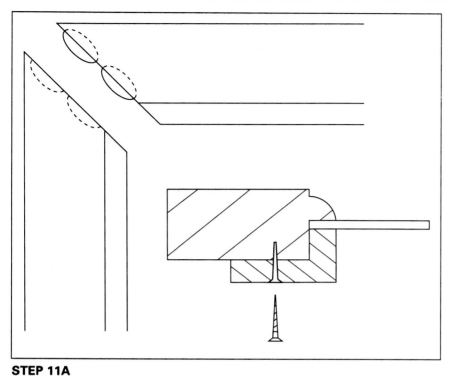

Make the Top

Cut a profile and rabbet into the inside edges of the top as shown in the drawing, then miter the corners. Join these miters with biscuits, as shown, or with dowels. Use ¼" plate glass in the top, and cut keepers as shown to hold it in from below with screws.

STEP 11A

Join the top corners with miters and biscuits as shown. Use dowels if you prefer. Miter the glass keeper at the corners, and place screws every 6" to hold the glass in tight.

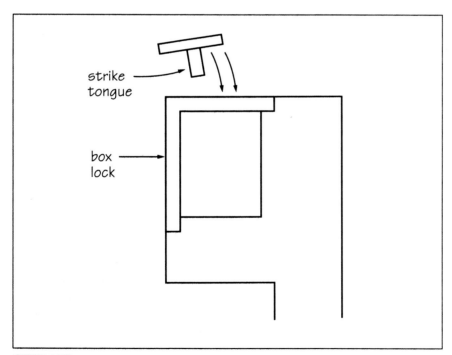

strike
tongue

box
lock

STEP 11B

Install a box lock if you wish to lock the tabletop. A box lock has a special strike plate with tongues that fit into the lock, which grabs onto them. Fit the strike plate into a mortise on the bottom face of the tabletop. Do so after you have installed the hinges.

CHAPTER TWO

DISPLAY CASES

Curved Top Display Case, Straight Top Display Case

The basic design and construction for this case is very similar to that of the display cabinet discussed in the next chapter. If you want to make both, do them at the same time—you'll find that many of the machine setups apply to both, with only minor changes. *Note: If you choose to use one of the molded sticking profiles for the glazed frames as described in chapter seven, you will need to change the order in which you do procedures for the frame joinery and for making the molded sticking on curved parts.* Those alternate procedures are detailed in part two of the book. Use the following step-by-step instructions *after* you have carefully planned the construction of your customized display case.

Curved Top Display Case

Follow the icons at the top of each page to identify part names, dimensions and construction steps for the display case you are making.

Straight Top Display Case

Follow the icons at the top of each page to identify part names, dimensions and construction steps for the display case you are making.

Display Case
Part Names

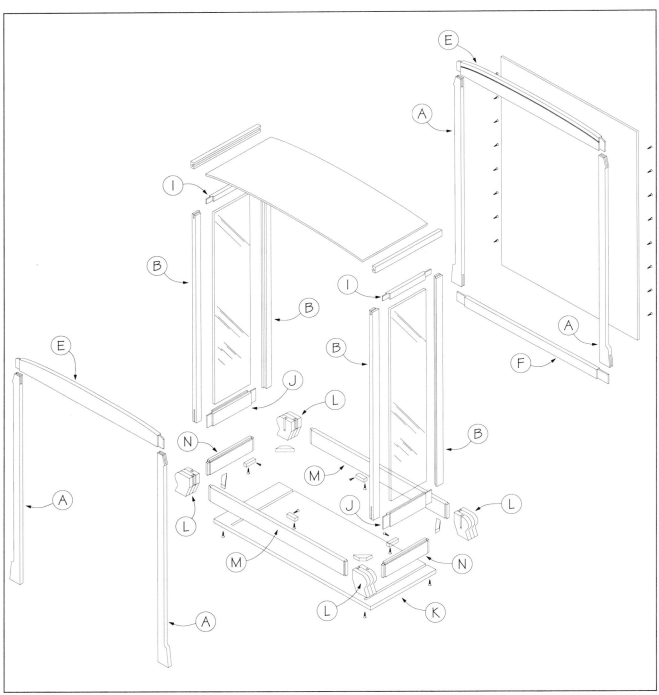

CASE

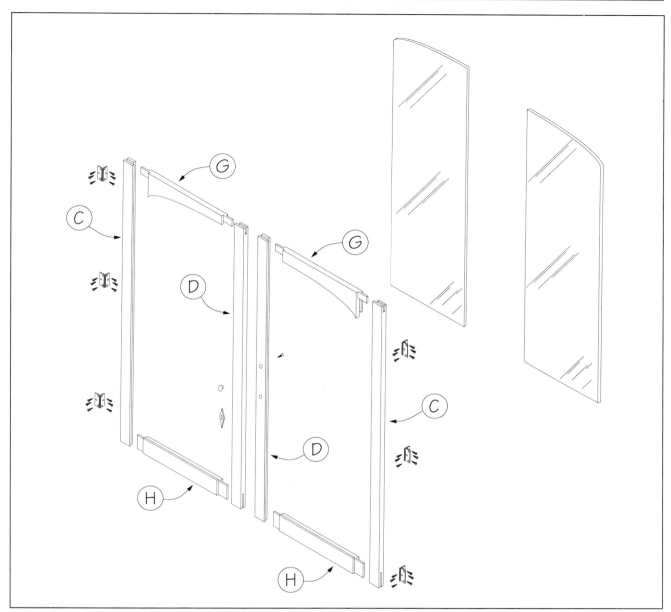

DOORS

PART NAMES—DISPLAY CASE

(A) front and rear frame posts
(B) side frame posts
(C) door hinge stiles
(D) door lock stiles
(E) front and rear frame top rails
(F) rear frame bottom rail
(G) door top rails

(H) door bottom rails
(I) side frame top rails
(J) side frame bottom rails
(K) bottom plate
(L) foot laminations
(M) bottom rails
(N) bottom rails

Curved Top Display Case
Dimensions

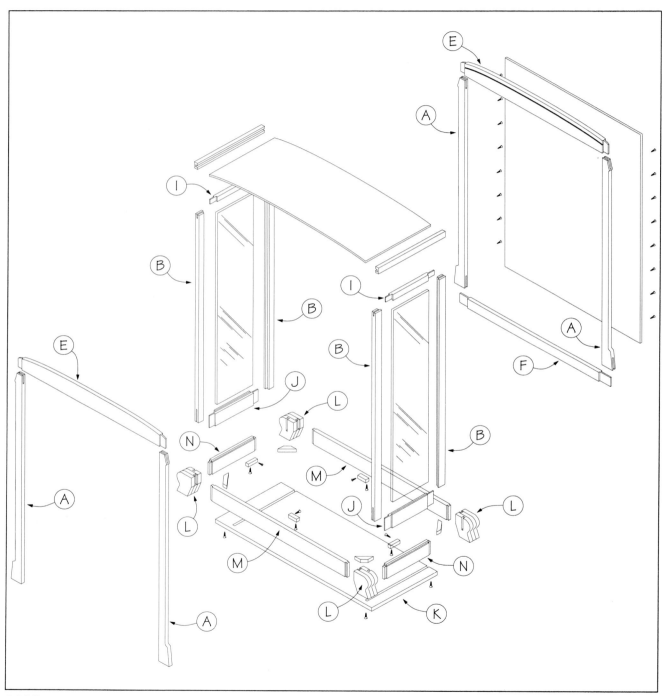

CASE

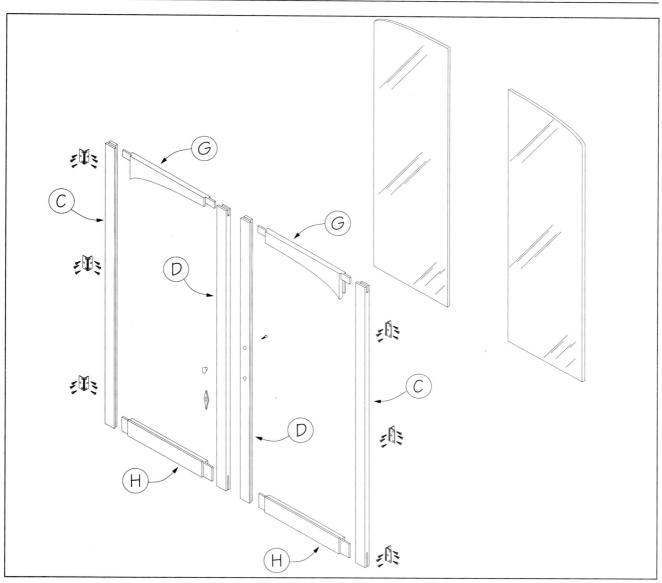

DOORS

CUTTING LIST—CURVED TOP DISPLAY CASE

³⁄₄″ stock:

4-2½×51¾	(A) front and rear frame posts
4-1¾×52	(B) side frame posts
2-1¾×50½	(C) door hinge stiles
2-1½×50½	(D) door lock stiles
2-4×41	(E) front and rear frame top rails
1-2¾×42	(F) rear frame bottom rail
2-4×18½	(G) door top rails

2-2¾×18½	(H) door bottom rails
2-2×13½	(I) side frame top rails
2-3×13½	(J) side frame bottom rails
1-15¾×43½	(K) bottom plate
12-4×5	(L) foot laminations
2-3½×38	(M) bottom rails
2-3×12¼	(N) bottom rails
1-¼×4′×8′	hardwood-veneer plywood for back and top.

Straight Top Display Case
Dimensions

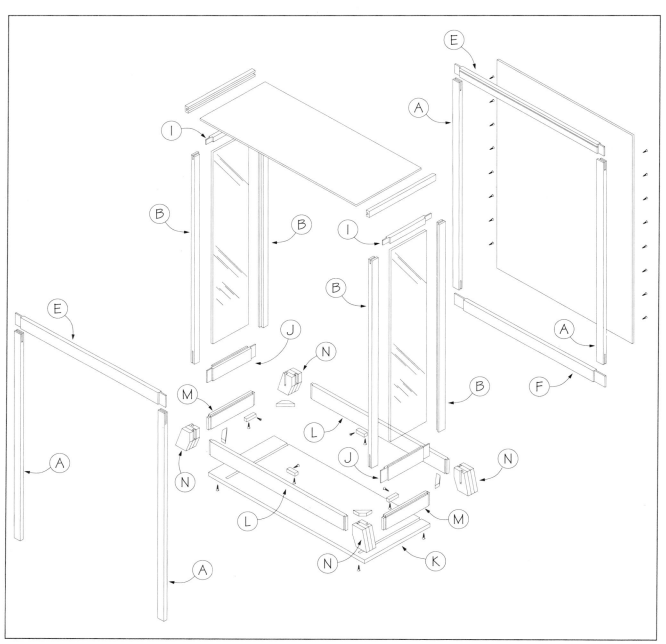

CASE

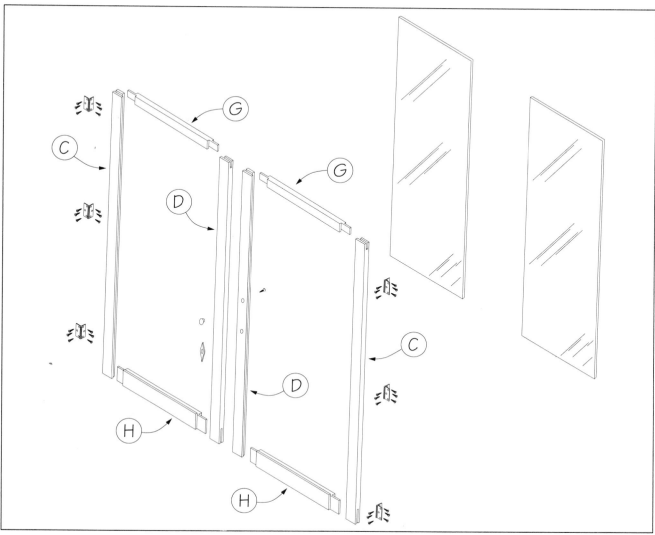

DOORS

CUTTING LIST—STRAIGHT TOP DISPLAY CASE

If you'd rather not futz around with curves, build the cabinet with all straight components as shown. The following cutting list is for the cabinet shown.

¾″ stock:

4-1½ × 52½	(A) front and rear frame posts		2-1½ × 13½	(I) side frame top rails
4-1¾ × 52½	(B) side frame posts		2- 2½ × 13½	(J) side frame bottom rails
2-1¾ × 51	(C) door hinge stiles		1-15¾ × 41½	(K) bottom plate
2-1½ × 51	(D) door lock stiles		2-2½ × 34½	(L) bottom rails
2-1½ × 40	(E) frame top rails		2-2½ × 12½	(M) bottom rails
1-2½ × 40	(F) rear frame bottom rail		12-4 × 5	(N) foot layers
2-1¾ × 18½	(G) door top rails		1-¼ × 4′ × 8′	hardwood-veneer plywood
2-2½ × 18½	(H) door bottom rails			for the back and top

Display Cases
Construction Steps

STEP 1

Making the Templates

Begin this project by making two plywood templates for flush trimming the curved parts. Quarter-inch-thick Baltic birch plywood is ideal for this, but other kinds will work well too (thicker plywood is OK). Don't use construction plywood—it has voids in it that can cause the template to break.

The first template is for the shaped edges of the posts on the front and rear frames. Enlarge and trace the design onto a piece of plywood and cut out the template on a band saw. Sand the curved edges of the template by hand or with a small drum sander at the drill press as shown at the top right. Straighten the edge of the long middle section of the template with a hand plane or sandpaper on a flat sanding block.

STEP 1A

A small drum sander mounted in the drill press is very handy for smoothing the curves on the template. These are available at most hardware stores.

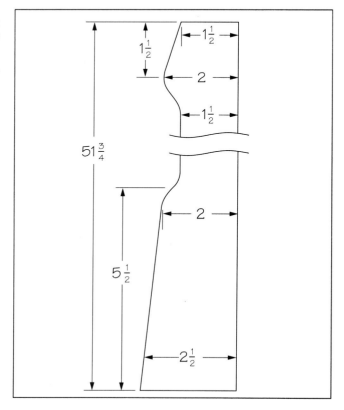

STEP 1B
Side Frame Template.

$51\frac{3}{4}$ $1\frac{1}{2}$ $1\frac{1}{2}$ 2 $1\frac{1}{2}$ 2 $5\frac{1}{2}$ $2\frac{1}{2}$

Using the Router Arcing Jig to Make Templates

Use a router arcing jig to make the arced template for the top rails of the front and rear frames of the cabinet, as well as the top rail doors. The jig is simply a plywood plate screwed to the router base, with a long arm attached to it. At the other end of the arm is a nail or screw driven into the table beneath for the jig to pivot upon. Use a ⅜" or ½" straight-flute carbide bit in the router to cut the plywood. Detailed plans for making this jig can be found in chapter eight.

Locate the pivot nail 77" from the *inside* of the router bit. Note that it is easy to adjust the distance between the two if the arm is made of two pieces clamped together, which can slide along each other to increase or decrease the length. Lay a piece of template plywood that is at least 15" × 40" on your bench top, with scrap plywood beneath for the bit to cut into. Secure these two to the bench top with clamps or small nails placed out of the way of the router bit and jig. Cut the top arc of the template.

Now locate the pivot nail 72" from the *outside* of the router bit. Use the same pivot hole that you used for the first cut, and cut the inside arc of the template. The resulting template will be 5" wide. As you make both cuts, be sure that the long arm of the jig stays straight by gently pulling the router away from the pivot point as you push along the arc. If the arm bends, the arc will not be smooth. Sand the template to remove irregularities and to smooth the edges.

Cut out Parts for the Frames

Now cut out all of the parts for the four frames and two doors as shown on the cutting list. Carefully pick very flat pieces for the meeting stiles on the doors. Note that you can cut the top rails for the front frame and doors from the same piece, so that the grain will be matched on these pieces. You can do the same for the front frame posts and door hinge stiles.

STEP 2
Cut the radii for the top rail arc template with an arcing jig and your router. Be sure that the long arm of the jig stays straight during the cut.

Choose Your Joinery

Follow the procedures outlined in chapter four for cutting square sticking with open mortise-and-tenon joinery for the side frames and doors. However, leave the door top rails rectangular and do not cut the glass rabbet yet; do cut the tenons as explained. Do not cut a glass rabbet on the front and rear frames at all, but simply use the tenoning jig to cut open mortise-and-tenon joints at the dimensions shown on the drawings. Note that the front frame has no bottom rail, but the rear frame does. Complete instructions to build the tenoning jig mentioned above can be found in chapter eight.

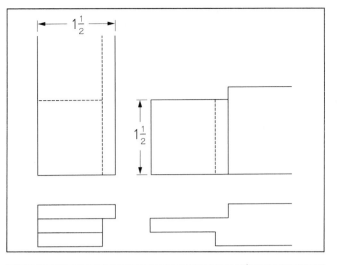

STEP 4A— BOTTOM DOOR FRAME JOINERY

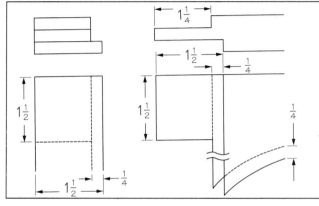

STEP 4B—TOP DOOR FRAME JOINERY (HINGE SIDE)

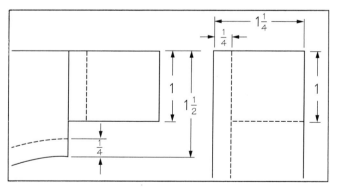

STEP 4C—TOP DOOR FRAME JOINERY

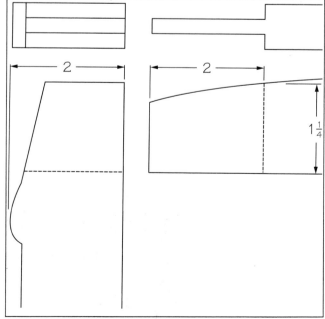

STEP 4D—FRONT TOP FRAME JOINERY

STEP 4E—BACK BOTTOM FRAME JOINERY

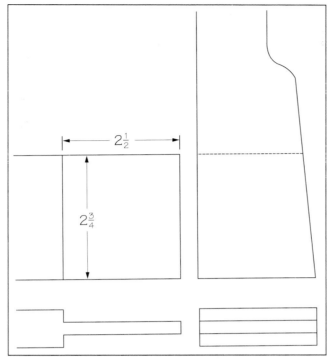

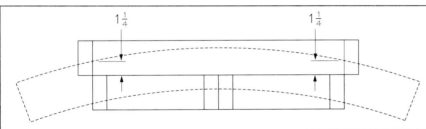

STEP 5—TOP RAIL TEMPLATE ALIGNMENT

After tenoning the top rails, place the door and front frame top rails together as shown. Make a template. Lay the template on top of them so that it covers 1¼" of the tenon shoulders on the frame top rail as indicated. Trace the curve.

STEP 6

Put the template on the backside of the rail, aligned to your scribe mark, and nail it down with small finish nails. Flush trim the rail to the template at the router table with a bearing-guided router bit.

Trace Pattern for the Curved Rails

Now use your curved top-rail template to trace the curve onto the top rails for the front and rear frames, as well as the door top rails. Make the tracing on the backside of each rail. Align the template to the parts as shown in the drawing labeled "Top Rail Template Alignment" at the center left. This drawing shows you how far the edge of the template should be from the straight edge of the parts, along the tenon shoulder. If you grain-matched the front rails, put them together with the grain aligned as shown in the drawing when you trace the curve.

Cut out the Curved Rails

Cut out the curves on all four rails on the band saw. Keep the cut about ⅛" to the waste side of the cut. Place the template on one of the rails aligned to the scribe mark, and attach it to the rail with small finish nails driven into the backside of the rail. Flush trim the rail to the template with a bearing-guided router bit at the router table as shown at the bottom left. Flush trim the other rails too.

Cut Rabbets for the Glass

Mount a ¼" bearing-guided rabbeting cutter into the router table as shown at the top right and cut a ½"-high glass rabbet into the inside edges of the two door top rails. Mark out the widths of the door top-rail tenons according to the dimensions on the drawings, and use a small handsaw to cut off the excess, as shown at the center right. Use a sharp chisel to clean up the sawn surfaces and bring the tenon to its correct size. The door top rails should now fit their stiles properly. *Note: You may need to trim just a bit off the cope shoulder as shown at the bottom right to make way for the stile sticking as it fits over the rail at this point.*

STEP 7A
Cut the glass rabbet into the inside edge of the curved top rails at the router table with a bearing-guided rabbet bit.

STEP 7B
Mark out the tenon widths and cut them to size with a handsaw, then clean up the surfaces with a sharp chisel.

STEP 7C
If necessary, trim a small amount from the cope shoulder on the top rails so that they fit onto the stiles.

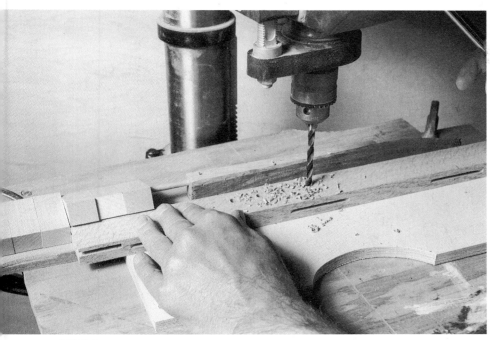

STEP 8

Bore holes for shelf keepers on the inside faces of the side frame posts. The holes on each post must be at uniform distances from the post bottoms so that the shelves line up well. A flipping spacer jig makes this fast and easy.

STEP 9

Use a biscuit joiner to cut slots for biscuit splines to join the side frames to the front and rear frames. Clamp fences to the bench edge to support the parts as they are cut.

STEP 8

Drill Holes for the Shelves

Bore ¼" holes ½" deep in the inside face of the side frame posts for shelf keepers. Be very careful to space the holes uniformly from the bottom of each post so that the shelves will contact all four keepers at the same height. You can bore the holes with a series of drill-press setups using a fence and end stop to accurately locate holes at each shelf level. The photo at the top left shows a special jig with flipping spacers that makes the work go faster. Locate the holes 1" apart, beginning at 10" above the bottom of each post and ending 10" from the top.

STEP 9

Make Cuts to Join Side Frame Posts to the Front Frame Posts

Use a biscuit joiner to cut slots in the edges of the side frame posts and the faces of the front and rear frame posts to join these components. You could use short dowels just as well. The photo (bottom left) shows a setup on a bench edge for making these cuts. Align the biscuits or dowels so that the inside faces of the side frames will be ¼" from the inside edges of the posts on the front and rear frames. Also, align the biscuits or dowels so that the side frames hang ¼" below the front and rear frames for the sliding dovetails on the side frames that fit into the bottom plate.

STEP 10

Trace Profile on the Posts

After cutting the biscuit joints, trace the profile of the front and rear frame-post template onto the four posts. Cut out the parts on the band saw, keeping the cut on the waste side of the line by ⅛″ or so. Attach the template to each post on the backside with small finish nails as you did for the top rails. Flush trim the edges as shown at the top right. Always keep your fingers away from the bit, and apply pressure downward on the part so that the bit does not grab and throw the part.

STEP 11

Cut a Curved Dado in the Top Rails of the Front and Rear Frames

Cut a curved dado in the top rails of the front and rear frames to accept the plywood top of the cabinet. Make this plywood top out of two pieces of ¼″ hardwood-veneer plywood placed together. Get the plywood at this point so that you can determine the exact thickness of two pieces placed together this way. Use a ¼″ or ⅜″ straight-flute bit at the router table to cut the dado as shown at the bottom right. Use a point-location fence to refer the cut along the curved edge of each rail as shown. Make two cuts; one for the top edge and one for the bottom edge of the dado. Adjust the fence location between cuts to arrive at the correct dado width, which should be just over the thickness of the two pieces of plywood. Make the dado ¼″ deep and ⅜″ from the edge of the rails.

STEP 10

Flush trim the front and rear frame posts to the template at the router table with a bearing-guided flush-trim bit. Attach safety handles to the template as shown to keep your fingers away from the cutter.

STEP 11A

Cut a dado along the inside edge of the front and rear frame rails for the plywood top. Since you must refer to a curved edge on the rails during the cut, use a point-location fence as shown.

STEP 11B—END CAP DETAIL

Cut the end caps at the table saw. Match the angle of the cut with the angle of the top groove at the point of intersection. Make the end cap groove a little wider than twice the thickness of your plywood.

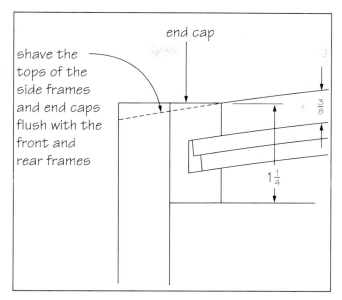

end cap

shave the tops of the side frames and end caps flush with the front and rear frames

$\frac{3}{8}$

$1\frac{1}{4}$

Glue up the Frames

Glue up the front, rear and two side frames, but not the doors. Be sure that the frames are square when glued up by comparing diagonal dimensions on the frames as shown below. Place C-clamps with glue blocks on the joints once the frames are square to pull the mortises onto the tenons. Make a temporary spacer rail 37" long for the front frame and clamp it in place near the bottom while you glue up the top joints. This makes it easy to align the top joints and check the frame for square.

STEP 12

Use just enough pressure from bar clamps to pull the joints together, but not enough to distort the parts. Pull the mortises onto the tenons with C-clamps and clamp blocks, then remove the bar clamps. Compare diagonal measures to check for square.

STEP 13

Use the Templates to Flush Trim the Joints

When the frames are out of the clamps, use your templates and a flush-trim bit in a handheld router to flush up the joints on the front and rear frames. This procedure is shown at the top right.

STEP 14

Cut the Sliding Dovetails

Cut sliding dovetails on the bottom edges of the side frames at the router table, as shown at the bottom right. These sliding dovetails will join the upper carcass to the bottom plate. Make a test dovetail slot in scrap to use when adjusting the width of the sliding dovetail on the bottom of the side frames. Use a dovetail bit that is ¾" wide at the widest point, and make the test slot ¼" deep. Adjust the width of the sliding dovetails so that they slide easily in the test slot but with a little slop. Make these dovetails ¼" high, and while you have this setup on the router table, cut the sliding dovetails on the tops of the two side base rails too.

STEP 13
After gluing up the frames, use the same templates that you used to make the curves to flush trim the edges of the joints. Clamp the template to the piece, and put your bearing-guided flush-trim bit in the router as shown.

STEP 14A
Install a vertical fence on your router table to support the side frames while you cut sliding dovetails on the bottom of the frames.

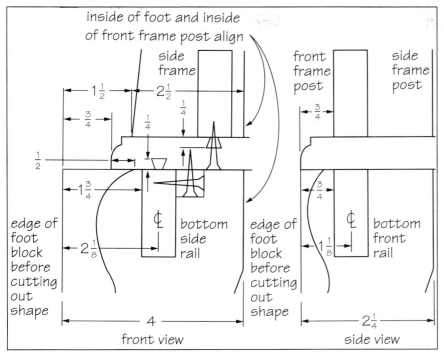

STEP 14B—BASE ASSEMBLY

Secure the bottom plate to the side frames with two screws on each side. Locate the screws about 3" apart, near the center of the plate rather than near the edges. This will allow the plate to move in response to moisture variations.

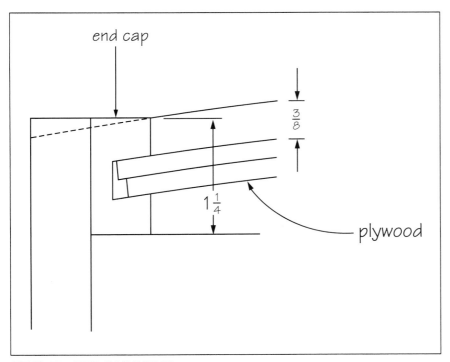

STEP 15—END CAP DETAIL

Cut the end caps at the table saw. Match the angle of the cut with the angle of the top groove at the point of intersection. Make the end cap groove a little wider than twice the thickness of your plywood.

STEP 15

Make the Top

Rip to width the two pieces of plywood for the top at 13^{15}⁄$_{16}$". Don't cut them to length yet. The ends of these pieces will fit into specially made end caps as shown in the drawing labeled "End Cap Detail" at the bottom left. Make these pieces now according to the dimensions on the drawing (or your variation), making their length equal to your side frame widths. Now dry fit the side frames to the front and rear frames with unglued biscuits (or dowels). Place one of the two top plywood pieces in the dado and trim its length to fit within the end caps. Cut the other to the same length, and practice fitting the plywood top pieces into place by bending them and pulling the frames together simultaneously. A second set of hands will help a great deal.

Glue up the Carcass

Once you are confident with fitting the top pieces in, glue up the carcass. Do not glue in the plywood top pieces, but do glue the end caps to the side frames. See below to locate and clamp end caps. Be sure to locate the side frames ¼" below the front and rear frames so that the dovetail shoulders are even with the bottoms of the frames. Place spacers in the glass rabbets of the side frames between the posts to prevent the frames from squeezing inward as they are clamped.

STEP 16A
Dry fit the carcass together before applying any glue to be sure that all parts line up.

STEP 16B
When you glue the frames together to form the carcass, place spacers within the side frames to take the pressure from the clamps as they squeeze the biscuit joints together. Otherwise, the posts will bend. Clamp the end caps to the side frames with C-clamps. Wash all extra glue away with hot water and a brush.

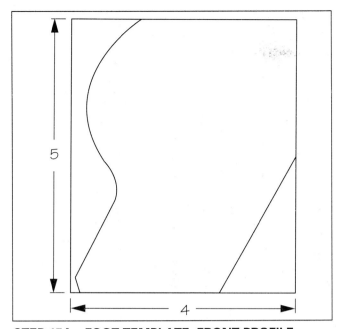

STEP 17A—FOOT TEMPLATE, FRONT PROFILE

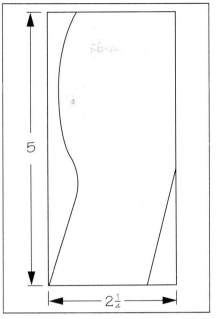

STEP 17B—FOOT TEMPLATE, SIDE PROFILE

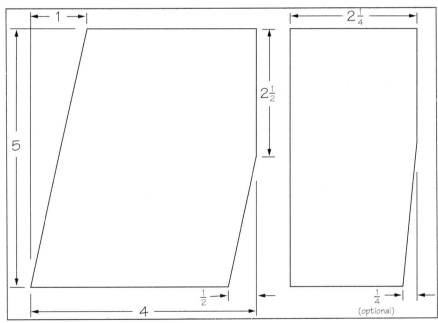

STEP 17C—ALTERNATIVE FOOT DETAIL

If you don't have a band saw, make your feet with straight angles as shown here. Cut the angles by hand or with a taper jig at the table saw.

STEP 17

Make the Feet

Make each of the four feet by gluing together three pieces of ¾"-thick lumber. Cut ½"-deep dovetail slots in these feet to join the base rails to them as shown on page 50 (top left). First cut smaller slots where the dovetail slots will go with a straight-flute bit to clear the waste, then use the dovetail bit. This precaution makes the dovetail cut easier. Trace the shape of the feet onto the glue blocks from the templates, and cut them out, as shown on page 50 (top right), on the band saw. Smooth the sawn surfaces by hand sanding, or with a scraper, which takes far less time.

STEP 17D

Before cutting the dovetails in the feet for the rails, first do the setup with a straight-flute bit to clear the waste. This makes less work for the dovetail bit and makes an easier, safer cut.

STEP 17E

Trace the foot templates onto each foot, and cut them out on the band saw. After you cut one side, tape the waste back on so the traced lines are there for you to cut to.

STEP 18

Make the Base Rails

Cut dovetails on the ends of the base rails with a setup like the one shown at the bottom right. Draw freehand curves on the bottom edge of these rails, cut them out on the band saw, and smooth the edges by sanding or scraping. Glue the base rails and feet together, square up the assembly, and screw in corner blocks as shown in the drawing. Remember that the sliding dovetails must protrude above the feet so that they will slide into the base plate.

STEP 18

Cut the sliding dovetails onto the tops of the base rails with the same setup that you used to cut dovetails onto the bottoms of the side frames.

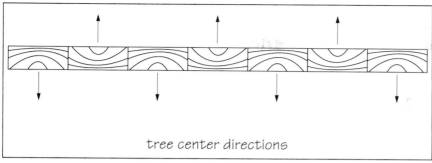

tree center directions

STEP 19A

When you edge glue stock together to make a wide plate, as with the bottom plate for this cabinet, arrange the pieces so that the direction of tree centers alternates between them as shown. This will minimize the effects of distortion as the wood cups from moisture variations.

STEP 19B

STEP 19

Make the Base Plate

Edge-glue pieces together for the base plate, and smooth the plate with a belt sander or hand plane. Cut dovetail slots in the base plate for the carcass and base as shown at the center left. Note that when you cut one direction, the bit pulls the router toward the fence; when you cut the other direction, it pulls away. Always cut in the direction that pulls toward the fence. To do so, you must start the cuts on two slots with a plunge cut near the front edge of the plate so that the slot won't be cut into the front edge itself.

The distance between the slots in the base plate is critical so that the base and carcass will fit. Slide the base and carcass onto the slots; do not glue them in place. This feature allows the base plate to move with moisture variations without affecting the carcass or base. Secure the carcass to the base with four screws placed in the center of the base plate, and secure the base to the base plate with screws and blocks.

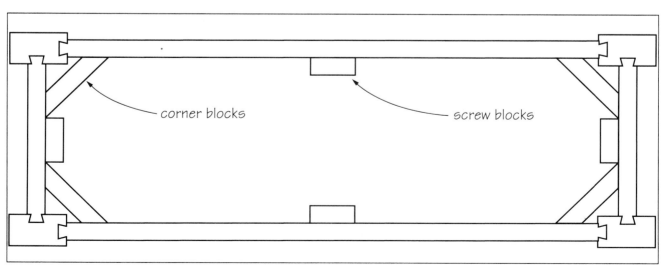

corner blocks — screw blocks

STEP 19C

DISPLAY CASES **51**

STEP 19D

Secure the bottom plate to the side frames with two screws on each side. Locate the screws about 3" apart, near the center of the plate rather than near the edges. This will allow the plate to move on the side frame dovetails in response to moisture variations. Note that the bottoms of the side frame posts and rails are flush, and both get the ¼" dovetail that holds them to the bottom plate.

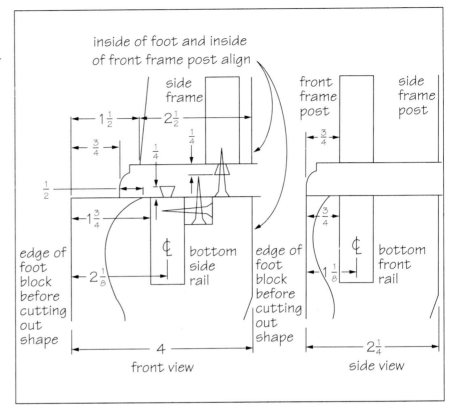

STEP 19E

The two top joints on the rear frame are identical to those on the front frame.

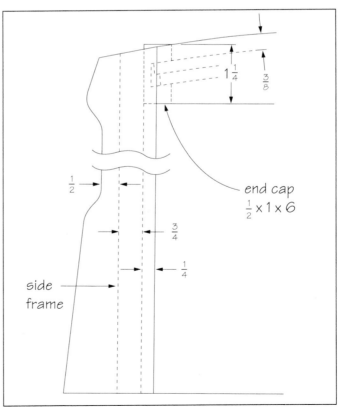

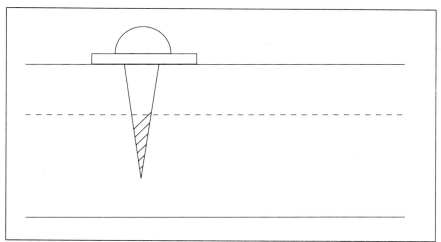

STEP 21

Secure the plywood back to the rear frame with roundhead screws and washers.

Fit the Side Frames and End Caps

Shave down the tops of the side frames and the end caps so that they fit flush with the front and rear side frames. Use a handsaw to make vertical cuts 1″ apart in the waste from front to rear. Knock out the bulk of the waste with a chisel, and use a hand plane or sandpaper to clean up the surface.

Cut a Rabbet for the Back

Use a router and a bearing-guided rabbeting bit to cut a rabbet ½″ wide and ¼″ deep in the back of the cabinet around the inside edge of the rear frame. Square the corners with a chisel, and fit a piece of ¼″ hardwood-veneer plywood into the rabbet. Use roundhead screws with washers placed every 6″ along the perimeter of the plywood to secure it to the rear frame. This plywood is an important structural element of the cabinet, giving it rigidity, and it must be well secured. Regular bevel-headed wood screws that are countersunk in the plywood would not be as strong, because a countersunk hole in ¼″ plywood can easily break. Roundhead screws with washers will hold better over the long haul.

Note that you can get all the ¼″ hardwood-veneer plywood for the project, including the back and the two pieces for the top, from one sheet.

STEP 22

Square up the Doors

Check the door opening for square. Glue up the doors and match their squareness to that of the opening. Hopefully all is perfectly square, but if the opening is badly out of square, you must set the square of the doors to match or else they won't fit.

STEP 23

Trim the Doors to Fit

When the doors are out of the clamps, trim them to fit with ¹⁄₁₆″ clearances all the way around. Trim them with a hand plane, or with small, careful cuts at the table saw. Glue a stop plate on the back of the left door for the other to contact. Install flush bolts on the left door to secure it in place, and install hinges and a lock as detailed in chapter eleven.

SUPPLIER LIST

Pre-made cabriole legs, as well as legs of other designs and complete furniture kits, can be had from:
   Adams Wood Products, 974 Forest Dr., Morristown, TN 37814. (615) 587-2942.

Hardware for cabinets is available from many mail order sources, and you will find most of them advertised in the woodworking magazines. Here is one such source:
   Whitechapel Ltd., P.O. Box 136, Wilson, WY 83014. (800) 468-5534.

For handtools and miscellaneous supplies, again look to the magazine advertisements for the various mail order houses. Here is one with a wide offering:
   Woodcraft, P.O. Box 1686, Parkersburg, WV 26102. (800) 225-1153.

Toggle clamps can be had from:
   De-Sta-Co, P.O. Box 2800, Troy, MI 48007. (800) 245-2759.

Almost all router bit manufacturers produce stile and rail bit sets for making kitchen cabinet doors with a groove for a solid panel. There are three basic types: solid, reversible stacking and two part stacking. The solid sets are not adaptable for glazed work. Some of the others are, but be certain when you order them that you get the necessary extra rabbeting cutter for making the glass rabbet. Reversible stacking sets, like that shown in the text, are less expensive because one set of cutters does the whole job. Two part sets cost more, but offer a wider range of sticking profiles to choose from. Listed here are two manufacturers of bits that offer a glazed joinery package:
   Eagle America, P.O. Box 1099, Chardon, OH 44024. (800) 872-2511.
   MLCS, P.O. Box 4053, Rydal, PA 19046. (800) 533-9298.

CHAPTER THREE

CURIO CABINETS

Curio Cabinet, Tall Curio Cabinet, Wide Curio Cabinet

This cabinet uses the same basic construction techniques as the floor-standing display case described in the previous chapter. To avoid a lot of duplication, I will refer you to pro-

cedural descriptions in chapter two for many of the procedures involved in making this cabinet. Read over that section to get the drift of building this design before turning back to

these pages. Use the following step-by-step instructions *after* you have planned the construction of your customized cabinet carefully.

Curio Cabinets

Follow the icons at the top of each page to identify part names, dimensions and construction steps for the curio cabinet you are making.

CURVED TOP

STRAIGHT TOP

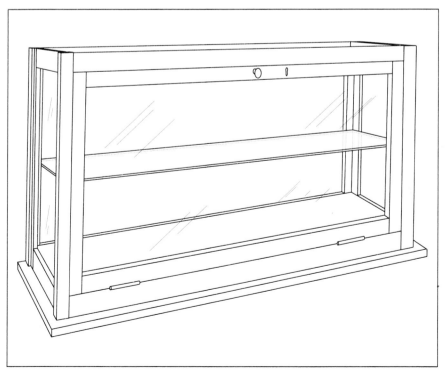

WIDE CURVED TOP

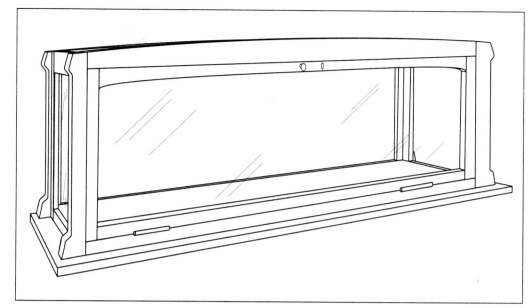

WIDE STRAIGHT TOP

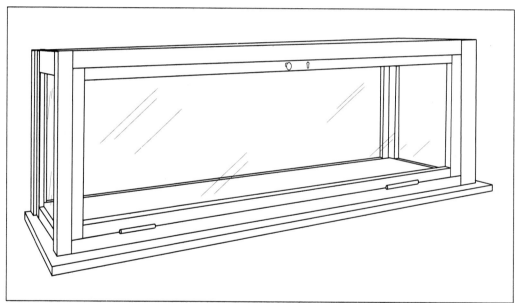

Curio Cabinets

Follow the icons at the top of each page to identify part names, dimensions and construction steps for the curio cabinet you are making.

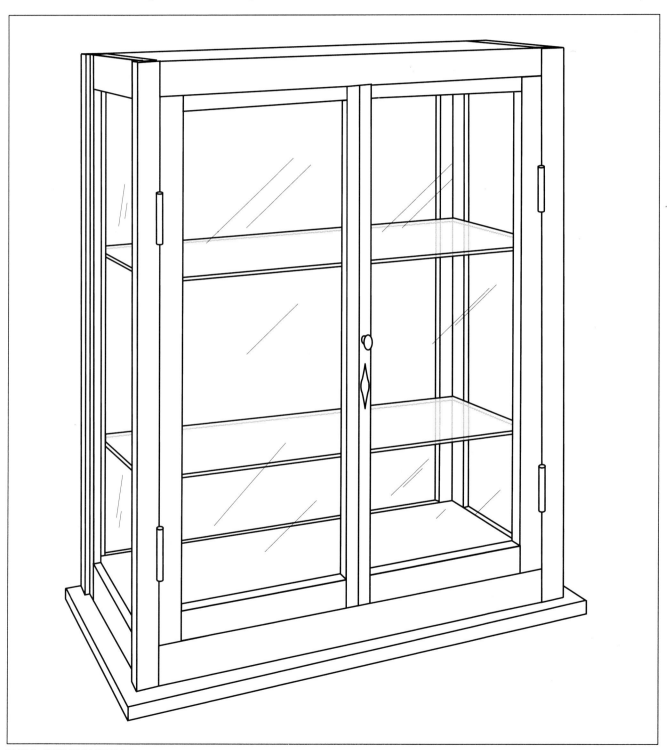

TALL STRAIGHT TOP

TALL CURVED TOP

Curio Cabinets
Part Names

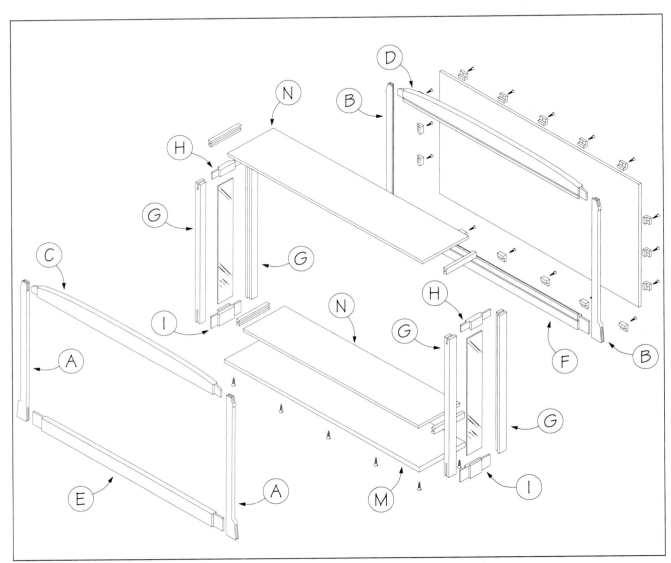

CABINET

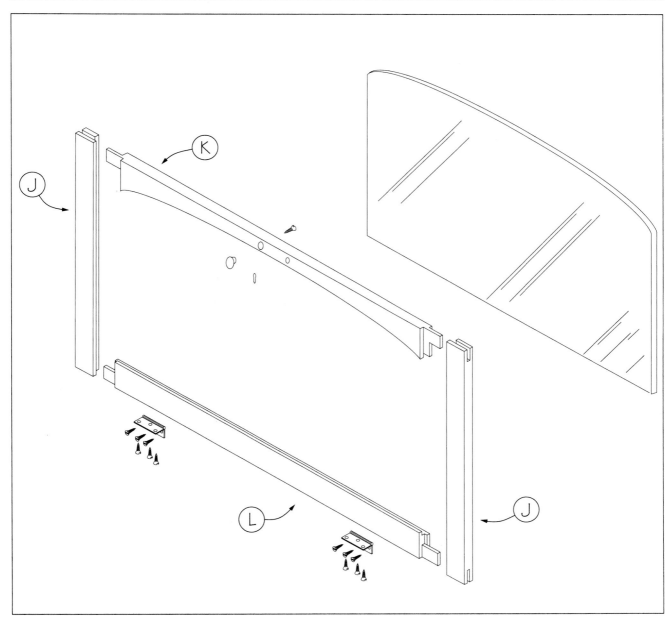

DOORS

PART NAMES—CURIO CABINETS

(A) front frame posts
(B) rear frame posts
(C) front frame top rail
(D) rear frame top rail
(E) front frame bottom rail
(F) rear frame bottom rail
(G) side frame posts

(H) side frame top rails
(I) side frame bottom rails
(J) door stiles
(K) door top rail
(L) door bottom rail
(M) bottom plate
(N) top and lower shelves

Curio Cabinet
Dimensions

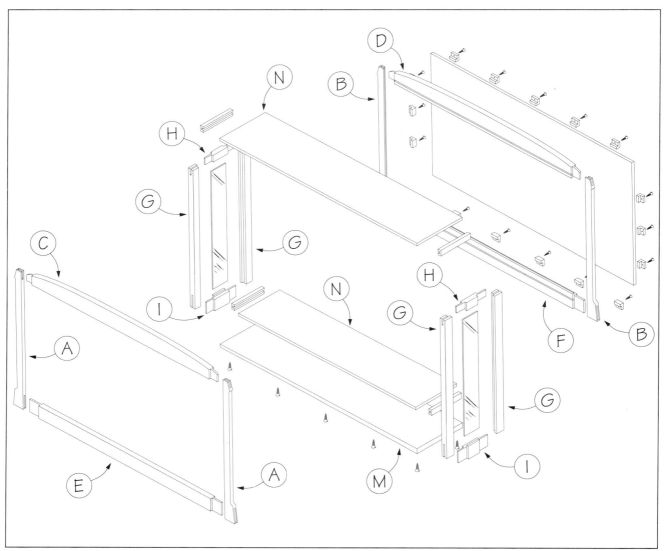

CABINET

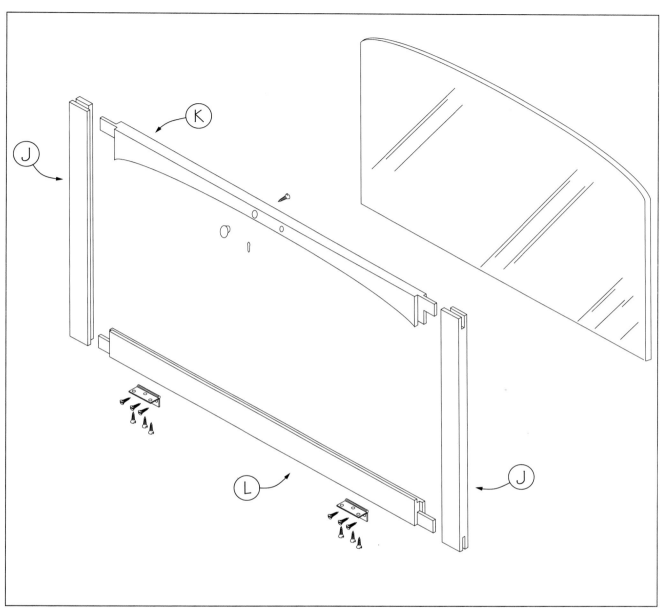

DOORS

CUTTING LIST—CURIO CABINET

¾" stock:

2-1⅝×25	(A) front frame posts
2-1⅞×25	(B) rear frame posts
1-2×38	(C) front frame top rail
1-2¼×38	(D) rear frame top rail
1-2×38¼	(E) front frame bottom rail
1-2¼×38¼	(F) rear frame bottom rail
4-1¼×25	(G) side frame posts

2-2×6	(H) side frame top rails
2-2¼×6	(I) side frame bottom rails
2-1½×22	(J) door stiles
1-2½×35	(K) door top rail
1-1¾×35	(L) door bottom rail
1-8×39¼	(M) bottom plate
2-¼×6¼×35	(N) top and lower shelves

plus whatever back you choose, small stock for end caps, etc.

Straight Top Curio Cabinet
Dimensions

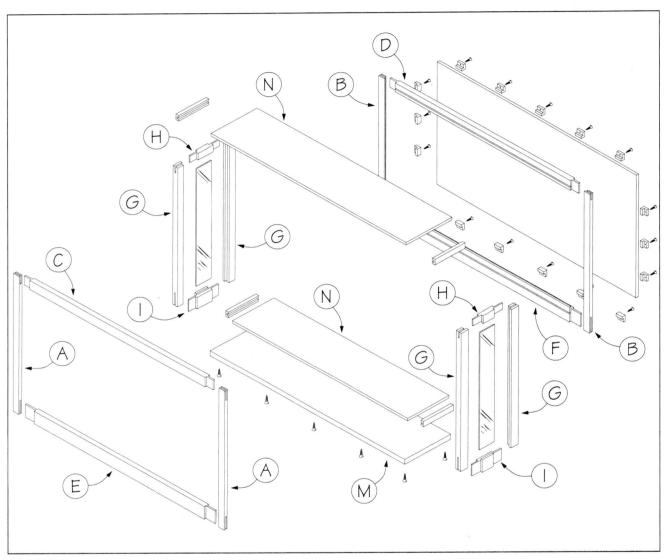

CABINET

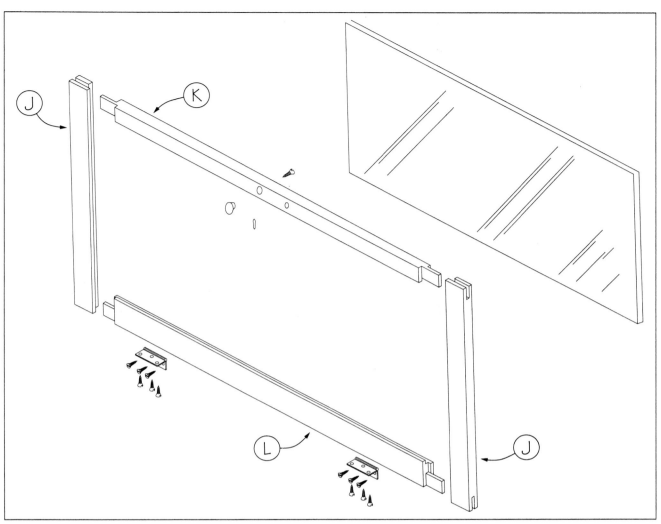

DOORS

CUTTING LIST—STRAIGHT TOP CURIO CABINET

If you prefer square designs to curves, or want to simplify the project, build it to these dimensions with the cutting list below.

¾″ stock:

2-1½ × 25	(A) front frame posts	2-2¼ × 6	(I) side frame bottom rails
2-1¾ × 25	(B) rear frame posts	2-1½ × 21½	(J) door stiles
1-1½ × 38	(C) front frame top rail	1-1¼ × 35	(K) door top rail
1-1¾ × 38	(D) rear frame top rail	1-1¾ × 35	(L) door bottom rail
1-2 × 38	(E) front frame bottom rail	1-8 × 39	(M) bottom plate
1-2¼ × 38	(F) rear frame bottom rail	2-¼ × 6¼ × 35	(N) top and lower shelves
4-1¼ × 25	(G) side frame posts		
2-1¾ × 6	(H) side frame top rails		

plus whatever back you choose; and small stock for end caps, etc.

Wide Curved Top Cabinet
Dimensions

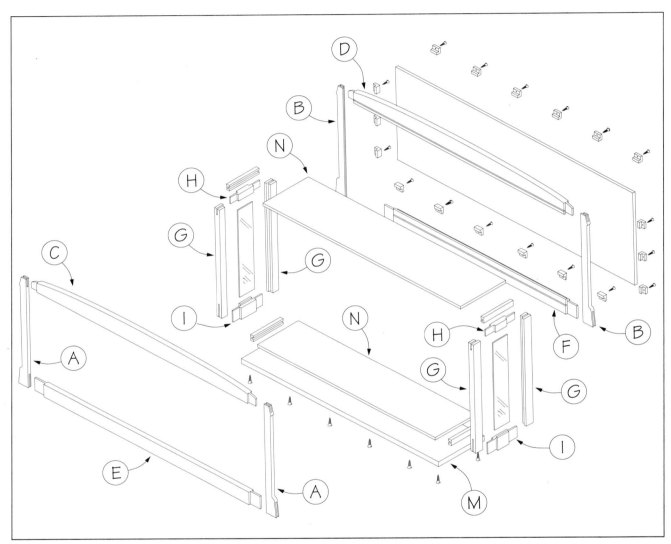

CABINET

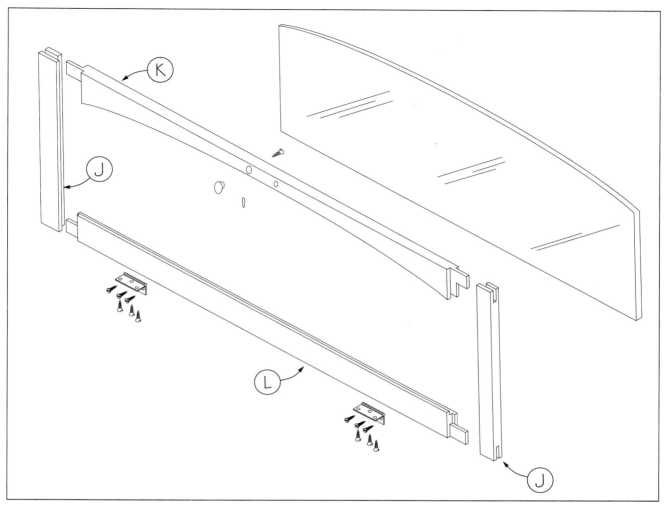

DOORS

CUTTING LIST—WIDE CURVED TOP CABINET

¾" stock:

2-1⅝ × 18	(A) front frame posts
2-1⅞ × 18	(B) rear frame posts
1-2 × 38	(C) front frame top rail
1-2¼ × 38	(D) rear frame top rail
1-2 × 38¼	(E) front frame bottom rail
1-2¼ × 38¼	(F) rear frame bottom rail
4-1¼ × 18	(G) side frame posts
2-2 × 6	(H) side frame top rails

2-2¼ × 6	(I) side frame bottom rails
2-1½ × 15	(J) door stiles
1-2½ × 35	(K) door top rail
1-1¾ × 35	(L) door bottom rail
1-8 × 39¼	(M) bottom plate
2-¼ × 6¼ × 35	(N) top and lower shelves

plus whatever back you choose, and small stock for end caps, etc.

Wide Straight Top Cabinet
Dimensions

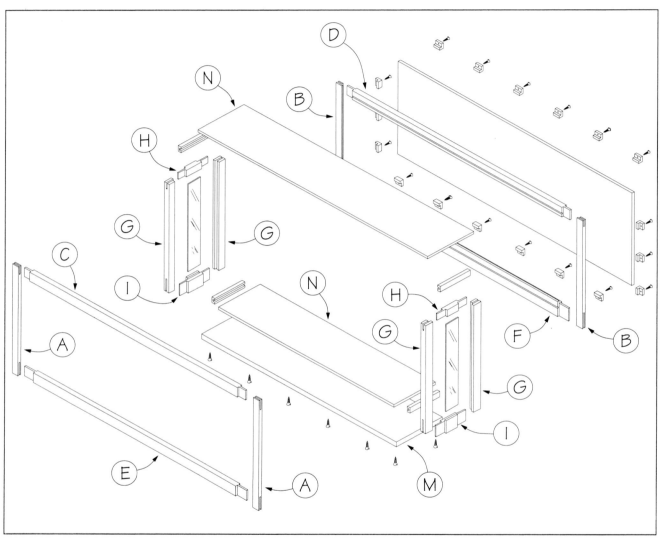

CABINET

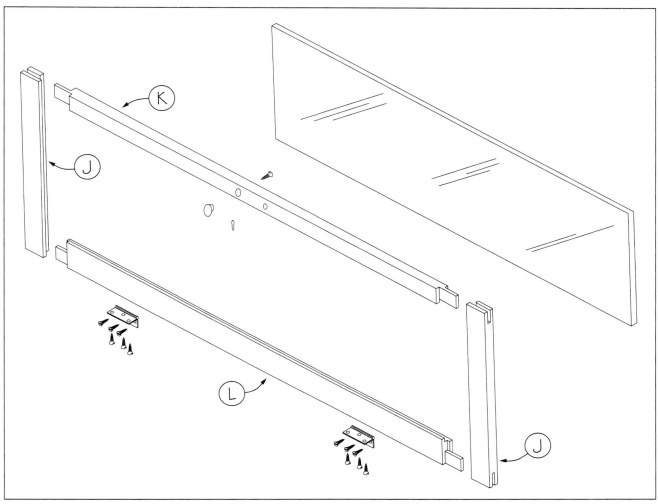

DOORS

CUTTING LIST—WIDE STRAIGHT TOP CABINET

¾″ stock:

2-1½ × 18	(A) front frame posts	2-2¼ × 6	(I) side frame bottom rails
2-1¾ × 18	(B) rear frame posts	2-1½ × 14½	(J) door stiles
1-1½ × 38	(C) front frame top rail	1-1¼ × 35	(K) door top rail
1-1¾ × 38	(D) rear frame top rail	1-1¾ × 35	(L) door bottom rail
1-2 × 38	(E) front frame bottom rail	1-8 × 39	(M) bottom plate
1-2¼ × 38	(F) rear frame bottom rail	2-¼ × 6¼ × 35	(N) top and lower shelves
4-1¼ × 18	(G) side frame posts	plus whatever back you choose, and small stock for end caps, etc.	
2-1¾ × 6	(H) side frame top rails		

Tall Cabinet With Curved Top
Dimensions

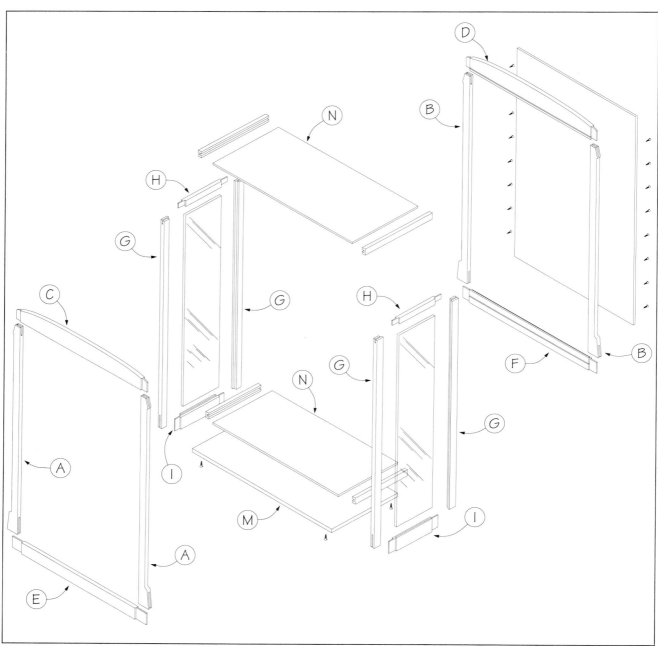

CABINET

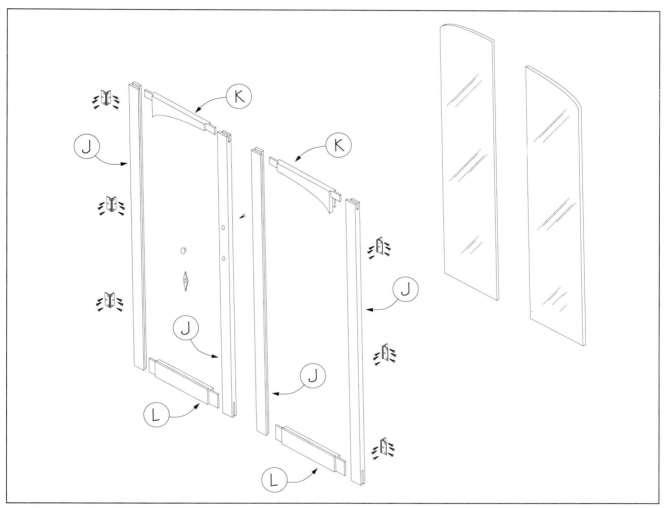

DOORS

CUTTING LIST—TALL CABINET WITH CURVED TOP

¾" stock:

2-1⅝ × 45	(A) front frame posts		4-1¼ × 42	(J) door stiles	
2-1⅞ × 45	(B) rear frame posts		2-2½ × 17½	(K) door top rail	
1-2 × 38	(C) front frame top rail		2-1¾ × 17½	(L) door bottom rail	
1-2¼ × 38	(D) rear frame top rail		1-10 × 39¼	(M) bottom plate	
1-2 × 38¼	(E) front frame bottom rail		2-¼ × 8¼ × 35	(N) top and lower shelves	
1-2¼ × 38¼	(F) rear frame bottom rail				
4-1¼ × 45	(G) side frame posts				
2-2 × 8	(H) side frame top rails				
2-2¼ × 8	(I) side frame bottom rails				

plus whatever back you choose, and small stock for end caps, etc. Note that this cabinet is large enough to stand on the floor, in which case you might choose to put feet and rails on it as in chapter two.

Tall Cabinet With Straight Top

Dimensions

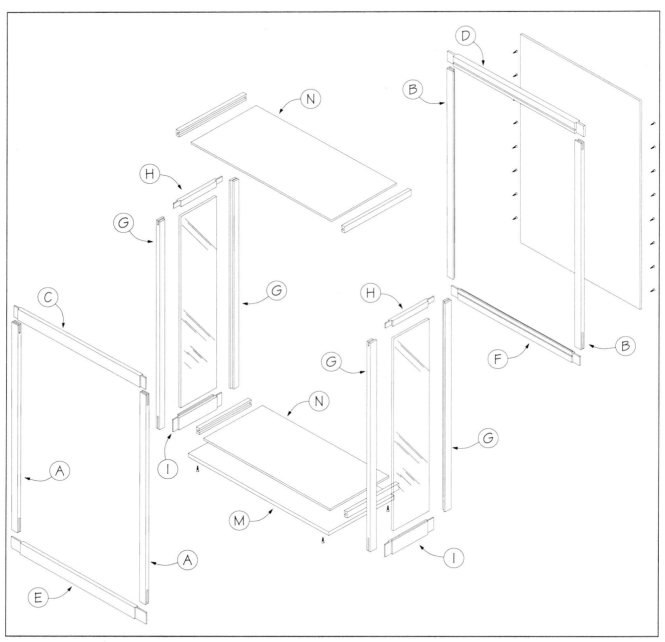

CABINET

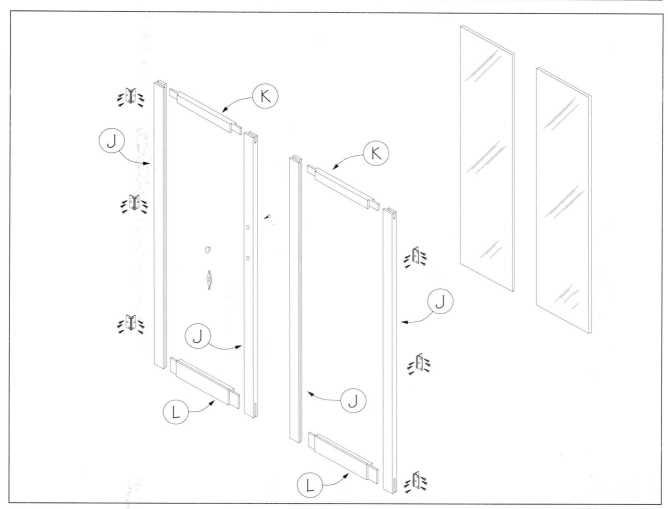

DOORS

CUTTING LIST—TALL CABINET WITH STRAIGHT TOP

¾″ stock:

2-1½×45	(A) front frame posts
2-1¾×45	(B) rear frame posts
1-1½×38	(C) front frame top rail
1-1¾×38	(D) rear frame top rail
1-2×38	(E) front frame bottom rail
1-2¼×38	(F) rear frame bottom rail
4-1¼×45	(G) side frame posts
2-1¾×8	(H) side frame top rails
2-2¼×8	(I) side frame bottom rails

4-1½×41½	(J) door stiles
2-1¼×17½	(K) door top rail
2-1¾×17½	(L) door bottom rail
1-10×39	(M) bottom plate
2-¼×8¼×35	(N) top and lower shelves

plus whatever back you choose, and small stock for end caps, etc. Note that this cabinet is large enough to stand on the floor, in which case you might choose to put feet and rails on it as in chapter two.

Curio Cabinets
Construction Steps

Make the Templates

Begin by making the two necessary flush-trimming templates; one for the posts on the front and rear frames, and one for the curved top rail. See photos at the right and below for the procedures involved. You'll find a drawing of the post template on page 75.

STEP 1A
A small drum sander mounted in the drill press is very handy for smoothing the curves on the template. These are available at most hardware stores.

STEP 1B
Cut the radii for the top rail arc template with an arcing jig and your router. Be sure that the long arm of the jig stays straight during the cut.

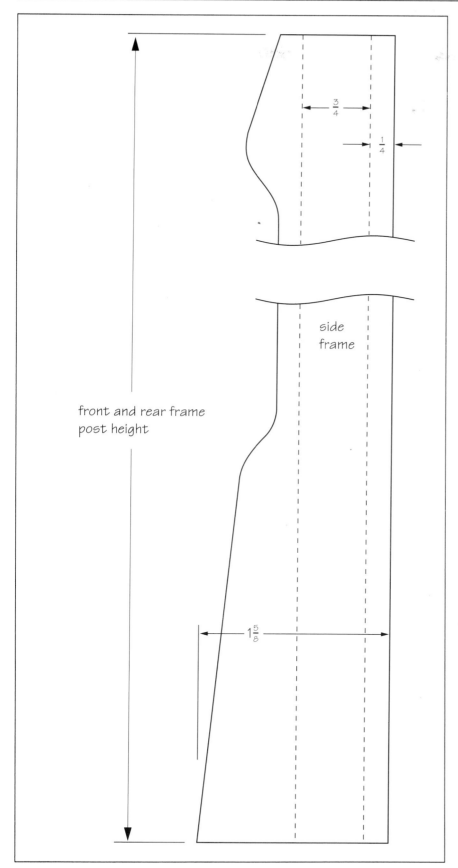

front and rear frame
post height

side
frame

$\frac{3}{4}$

$\frac{1}{4}$

$1\frac{5}{8}$

Make the Curved Top Template

For the curved top-rail template, use a radius of 13' for the top of the template. Measure 13' from the router-jig pivot nail to the inside of the router bit. For the lower edge of the template, use a radius of 12'9". Measure this distance from the pivot to the outside of the router bit when setting up the jig.

Plan Grain Matching for the Cabinet Front

Now get out all of your parts for the cabinet frames according to the cutting list. Notice that you have excellent opportunities for attractive grain matching on the front of the cabinet. If your stock is wide enough, get all the adjacent parts from common pieces. Mark them so that you know where the grain matches. For instance, if you get a door stile and its adjacent front frame post from the same piece, make a pencil mark across the two to show where they join. This mark will prevent you from accidentally flipping one of the parts and ruining the grain match.

STEP 1C—SIDE FRAME TEMPLATE, CURIO CABINET.

Choose the Joinery

Follow the instructions in chapter four for cutting the open mortise-and-tenon joints as well as the square sticking on the frame parts. Use the drawings to get the specific dimensions of each set of joints. Remember, the joinery is up to you. There are a few differences between the cabinet design in this chapter and that in chapter two. First of all, the rear frame on these cabinets gets cope and stick joinery, whereas those in chapter two do not. The only frame in the cabinets in this chapter that does not get cope and stick joinery is the front frame, which the door fits into. Another major distinguishing feature of the cabinet design in this chapter is the front frame bottom rail and lower shelf, both of which are absent on the design presented in chapter two.

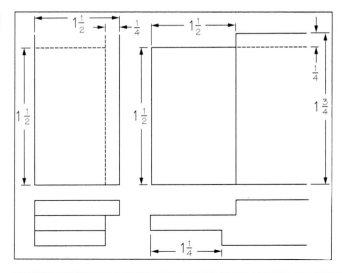

**STEP 4A—
DOOR BOTTOM
JOINERY**

**STEP 4B—
DOOR TOP
JOINERY**

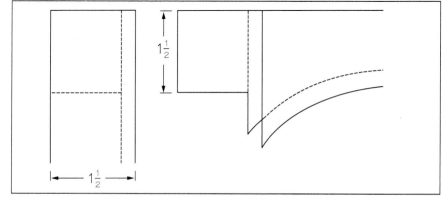

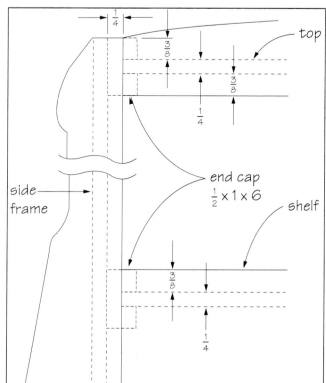

**STEP 4C—
TOP AND
SHELF
ALIGNMENT**

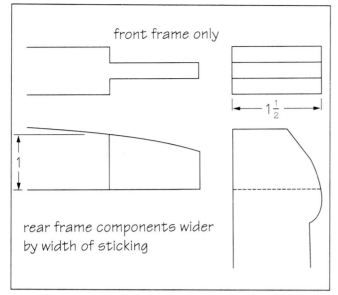

STEP 4D—FRAME TOP JOINERY

front frame only

1½

1

rear frame components wider
by width of sticking

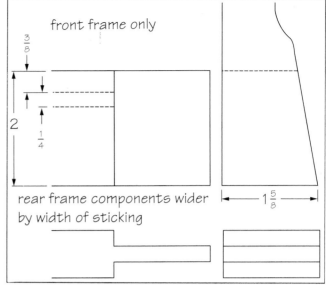

STEP 4E—FRAME BOTTOM JOINERY

front frame only

3/8

2

1/4

rear frame components wider
by width of sticking

1⅝

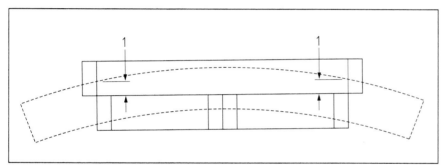

1   1

STEP 5A—TOP RAIL TEMPLATE ALIGNMENT

To trace the curve of the template onto the door and front frame top rails, first align the two rails together as shown. Place the template onto the rails so that 1" of the tenon shoulders of the frame top rail is covered as shown, and trace the curve. The front frame and rear frame are not exact duplicates of each other. Joints for the rear frame resemble those of the door bottom rail. Unlike the front frame, the rear frame has sticking and a rabbet. Dimensions for the rear frame joints are the same as those for the front frame joints except that the parts are ¼" wider toward the inside. This extra ¼" is the sticking. Note that the finished internal dimensions of the rear frame are both ½" less than those of the front frame, due to the sticking. The rabbets of the rear frame should line up with the inside edge of the front frame. Another way to look at it is that the rear frame is a duplicate of the front, except that it has a ¼" sticking added on the inside.

STEP 5

Align the Top Rail

The other major difference is where the top rail template is aligned to the two top rails. After cutting the tenons on all rails, place the front frame top rail and the door top rail together in position on a table as shown in the drawing labeled "Top Rail Template Alignment" (bottom left). Place the rails with the insides facing up. Put the template on them so that it is 1" above the bottom of the tenon shoulders on the front frame rail, as shown in the drawing. For the rear frame top rail, locate the template 1" above the glass rabbet, not above the lower edge of the sticking. Now scribe the template line on both the rails, and proceed with cutting the curves, flush trimming the edges, etc., as described in chapter two.

STEP 6

Bore Holes for the Shelves

Bore holes for shelf keepers in the side frame posts as described in chapter two and shown at the top right.

STEP 7

Join Sides to the Front and Back

Cut biscuit joints into the edges of the side frame posts and inside faces of the front and rear frame posts to join the side frames to these other frames. Set up on your bench edge with a supporting fence as shown at the center right to cut these biscuit slots. If you prefer, use dowels to join these parts. Note that the side frames come flush to the bottom of the other frames, unlike the floor cabinet where they are offset because of the sliding dovetails. Locate the inside face of the side frames ¼″ from the inside edges of the front frame posts, but ½″ from the inside sticking edge of the rear frame posts.

STEP 8

Flush Trim the Rear and the Front Frame Posts

Flush trim the front and rear frame posts to the post template as shown at the bottom right. Attach dowels to the template to make the procedure safer, since the parts are small. Note that the rear frame posts are wider than the front frame posts by ¼″, the width of the square sticking. Align the template to the rabbet edge on the rear posts, not the sticking edge.

STEP 6
Bore holes for shelf keepers on the inside faces of the side frame posts. The holes on each post must be at uniform distances from the post bottoms so that the shelves line up well. A flipping spacer jig makes this fast and easy.

STEP 7
Use a biscuit joiner to cut slots for biscuit splines to join the side frames to the front and rear frames. Clamp fences to your bench edge to support the parts as they are cut.

STEP 8
Flush trim the front and rear frame posts to the template at the router table with a bearing-guided flush-trim bit. Attach safety handles to the template as shown to keep your fingers away from the cutter.

STEP 10

Use a straight-flute bit at the router table, or a dado set at the table saw, to cut grooves in the front and rear frame top and bottom rails to accept the cabinet top and lower shelf.

STEP 11A

Use just enough pressure from bar clamps to pull the joints together, but not enough to distort the parts. Pull the mortises onto the tenons with C-clamps and clamp blocks, then remove the bar clamps. Compare diagonal measures to check for square.

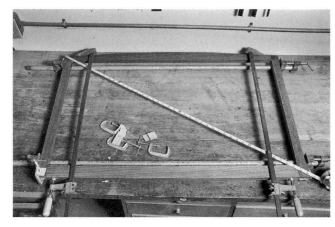

STEP 11B

By far the fastest way to level joints is with hand tools like planes and scrapers. Rough sandpaper works well too, but then you must work through finer grits to smooth the surface. Planes and scrapers leave a smooth surface to begin with.

Make the Top

Decide what material you will use for the cabinet top and lower shelf. Quarter-inch hardwood-veneer plywood will work well here, or solid wood planed to ¼" thickness.

Cut Grooves for the Top

Cut grooves for the cabinet top and lower shelf into the top and bottom rails of the front and rear frames as shown at the top left. This can also be done just as well at the table saw with a dado set. Adjust the width of this groove to the thickness of the top and shelf. Make the groove ¼" deep, and ¼" from the inside edge of the front frame rails, but ½" from the inside sticking edge of the rear frame rails.

Glue up the Frames

Glue together the frames (but not the door yet), checking for square by comparing diagonals as shown at the center left. Equal diagonals denote a square frame. Use C-clamps to pull the mortises onto the tenons as shown. When out of the clamps, scrape the joints flush, as shown at the bottom left, or sand them flush. Flush trim the joints on the front and rear frames as shown on page 80 (top left), using a bearing-guided flush-trim bit in your router as shown, and the templates clamped flush to their corresponding curved surfaces.

STEP 11C

After gluing up the frames, use the same templates that you used to make the curves to flush trim the edges of the joints. Clamp the template to the piece, and put your bearing-guided flush-trim bit in the router as shown.

STEP 12A

Dry fit the carcass together before applying any glue to be sure that all parts line up.

STEP 12

Make the End Caps

Make end caps for the cabinet top and lower shelf as shown on page 76 (bottom right). Cut the top and shelf to width and length, and dry fit the carcass together with the end caps, top and shelf, as shown at the center right, to be certain all aligns well. Glue the carcass together as shown at the bottom right, making sure the side, front and rear frames all line up at the bottom. Don't glue in the top and shelf, but glue the end caps to the side frames.

STEP 13

Fit the Frames

Shave down the tops of the side frames and the end caps so that they fit flush with the front and rear side frames. Use a handsaw to make vertical cuts 1" apart in the waste from front to rear. Knock out the bulk of the waste with a chisel, and use a hand plane or sandpaper to clean up the surface.

STEP 12B

When you glue the frames together to form the carcass, place spacers within the side frames to take the pressure from the clamps as they squeeze the biscuit joints together. Otherwise, the posts will bend. Clamp the end caps to the side frames with C-clamps.

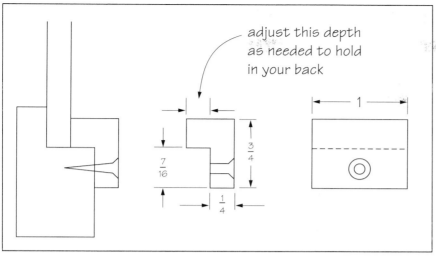

adjust this depth as needed to hold in your back

$\frac{7}{16}$

$\frac{3}{4}$

$\frac{1}{4}$

1

STEP 17A—KEEPER DETAIL

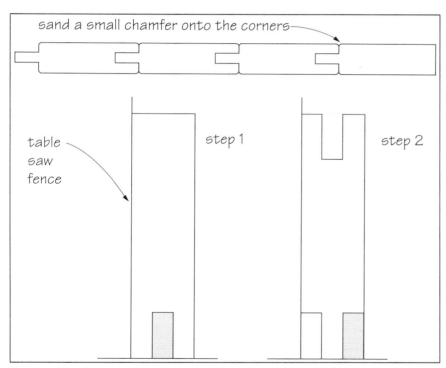

sand a small chamfer onto the corners

table saw fence

step 1

step 2

STEP 17B—TONGUE AND GROOVE PANELING ALTERNATIVE FOR CABINET BACK

Cut out pieces at ⅜" thick by whatever widths you have. Cut a groove at the table saw as shown in Step 1, and the tongue as in Step 2. Hold each panel slat in the cabinet back with one keeper at each end.

STEP 14

Glue up the Bottom Plate

Edge-glue pieces together for the bottom plate, and cut a detail into its edge with your router. Screw this plate to the frame bottom rails, and cover the screws with wood plugs.

STEP 15

Glue up the Door

Check the door opening for square. Glue up the door and match its squareness to that of the opening. Hopefully all is perfectly square, but if the opening is badly out of square, you must set the square of the door to match or it won't fit.

STEP 16

Install Door Stops

Glue two small triangles in the upper inside corners to stop the door from swinging inward, and you are ready to fit the door to the opening with a hand plane, or at the table saw, and to install hardware.

STEP 17

Make the Back

For the back, use hardwood-veneer plywood, a mirror, plywood covered with cotton sackcloth (use regular wood glue and clamp it down with weights), or make ⅜" thick tongue-and-groove paneling as shown in the drawing. Hold the back in with small keepers as shown at the top left.

Install the Shelves

For shelves use ¼" plate glass, which you can order from a glass supply. Have them grind the edges so they are not sharp. Remember that glass shelves of this length will not support very heavy objects.

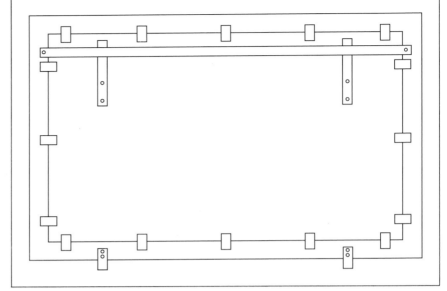

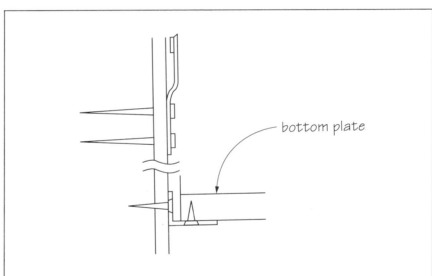

STEP 18

Hanging the Cabinet on the Wall. Buy ⅛" × 1" metal strapping at the hardware store. Cut two 6" long pieces, and shape them as hooks as shown. Screw a long strap to the cabinet back. Screw the hooks and L brackets to wall studs, not to wall board alone. Adjust the heights so that the weight of the cabinet rests on the L brackets, and the hooks prevent it from tipping forward. Use two sets of hooks and brackets, and secure the cabinet to two separate wall studs—one isn't enough.

PART TWO

TECHNIQUES

Techniques

Building glazed cabinets is one of the finer aspects of woodworking, but it doesn't have to be one of the most difficult. The techniques in this section show you in detail three different ways to make wooden frames for glass, as well as a variety of other possibilities. Of the three primary techniques shown here, the first, square sticking, is very easy to do and requires only a table saw. The second, mitered sticking, and third, router cope and stick, are more elaborate because they use a molded profile on the frames. Mitered sticking joins this molded profile with an age-old hand-tool technique that is surprisingly easy. Router cope and stick uses modern, specialized router bits in a router table with a procedure similar to that used by professionals to make kitchen cabinet doors.

These three techniques—square sticking, mitered sticking, and router cope and stick—cover a wide range of territory for building glazed cabinets, and the other techniques show you more alternatives. This section also includes various jigs and information that will help you vary the design of your particular cabinet. Other information includes plans and instructions for a tenoning jig, a router arcing jig for curved rails, cutting closed mortises, and techniques for cutting and installing glass, as well as finish work.

The techniques presented here are directly applicable to the designs for the display cabinets in the first part of the book, and give you the information you need to make those cabinets using a molded profile on the frames. You will also find these techniques and instructions useful in other woodworking applications. Thus, with this book you can choose what techniques suit your taste, tooling and preferred working methods, and apply them to one of the given designs or one of the variations on those that are shown. Or you can design your own cabinet and use these techniques to give you the details you need to make the frame joinery involved.

Glazing and Cabinetry

Let's take a close look at the basic task at hand. Glass must be put into a rabbet, rather than a groove like a wood panel, so that it can be replaced when it breaks. A rabbet is easy to make, but how do you join two rabbeted pieces at a corner joint so that all the surfaces connect tightly? This is the basic problem of glazed frame joinery, and there are numerous solutions.

Glazing Terminology

First let's look at a little terminology for glazed frames. The vertical components are often called *posts* when they are integral with the cabinet, and *stiles* when they are on doors. Between these posts or stiles are *rails*, which butt up against the inside edges of the posts and stiles. Along the inside of the frame is a *rabbet* which faces toward the middle of the cabinet. The *sticking* is the inside edge of the frame parts not removed by the rabbet—the lip left by the rabbet holds the glass. It faces toward the outside of the cabinet and is highly visible.

Because the sticking is highly visible, woodworkers often want to put a molded profile on it to give the frame an attractive, detailed appearance. But now you have to join not only a rabbet, but also a molded profile with no gaps at the frame corners. It's easy to join the pieces when the sticking is square by simply cutting another rabbet, or *cope*, on the end of the rail to make way for the sticking on the joining part. That's the solution presented in the first of the three principal techniques covered here, as well as in part one of the book.

To join molded sticking, you must get a bit fancier. One traditional way of doing this is to miter the sticking with a chisel and a jig, producing a very tight joint. This is the second of the three methods covered here. This technique, while effective, is a bit time-consuming, so professionals have developed machine techniques that speed up the process. Various "stile-and-rail" router bits are available for doing cope-and-stick joinery on kitchen cabinet doors, and some of these are easily adaptable for making a glass rabbet. This is the third principal method covered here.

Joinery Dimensions

There's one rather confusing aspect to this kind of work that I want you to think about early on. Every glazed frame has a rabbet around the inside,

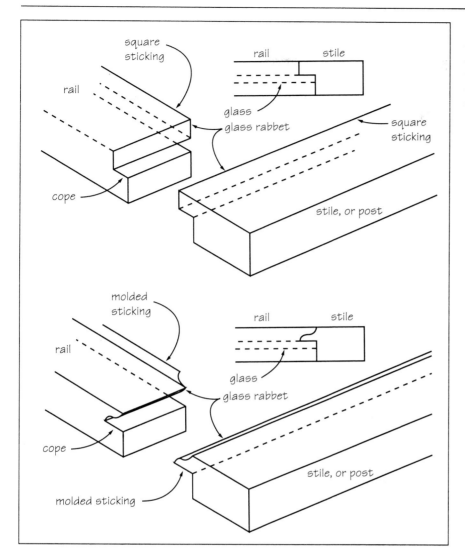

COPE AND STICK

Illustrated here is the "cope-and-stick" method of joining stiles and rails. With either a square or molded sticking, make a cope cut on the rail end which fits snugly over the sticking on the stile edge.

which creates two separate width dimensions to deal with. The first is the total width of the part, including the sticking. The second is the width of the part minus the sticking, or the width of the part from the outer part edge to the rabbet. This is called the face width.

When you design a cabinet with such frames you must pay close attention to when you use each of these two widths. The length of rails, for instance, must be figured between rabbets, not between sticking edges, when you use the router cope

and stick technique in chapter seven. If you use a sticking of a different width than that discussed in previous chapters (¼"), you must adjust the total width of your parts to compensate. You want the face width to remain the same, so the total width must be increased or decreased by the difference in the sticking. Carefully alter the cut list widths given if you choose a different sticking.

Notice also that you must change the location from the sticking edge of the grooves for the top and lower shelves in the cabinets of chapter

three if you change the sticking. This applies only to the rear frame, which has sticking, but not to the front frame, which does not. The grooves in the front and rear frames must be at the same height when all is said and done.

The following information presumes that you will be using ¾"-thick lumber (or ¹³⁄₁₆" as it often comes). Many of these techniques are applicable to other dimensions, but ¾" thickness is a good basis for most cabinet frames.

CHAPTER FOUR

SQUARE STICKING—OPEN MORTISE-AND-TENON JOINERY

This method of joining the sticking at the corners is very easy and requires only a table saw. It is also rather plain looking in contrast to the molded sticking obtained by the other methods covered later.

STEP 1

Cut the Parts to Length

Rip your parts to width and cut them to length. Now cut a rabbet into the edge of all parts that will have glass put into them. You can cut this with a dado set on the table saw, or with a rabbeting cutter at the router table.

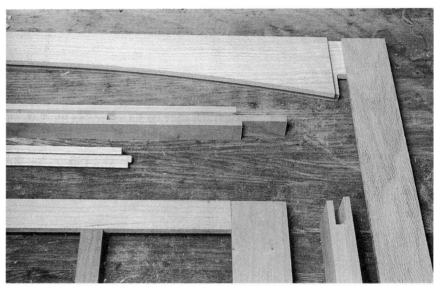

COPE AND STICK

STEP 2

Cut the Open Mortises

Next, cut open mortises into the ends of the stiles. Cut these mortises using a table-saw jig as shown at the bottom right. Detailed plans and construction instructions can be found in chapter eight. Make the mortises one-third the width of your stock, and centered along the thickness of the parts. Center the mortise by flipping the part between cuts.

CUTTING OPEN MORTISES ON FRAME STILES WITH A TABLE-SAW TENONING JIG

CUTTING TENONS ON FRAME RAIL WITH THE TABLE-SAW TENONING JIG

STEP 3

Cut the Tenon Shoulders

Now set up your miter gauge at 90° with a wood extension fence screwed onto it. Clamp an end stop to the fence. Use this setup to cut tenon shoulders on the rails. Set the distance from the end stop to the other side of the blade equal to the length of the tenons you desire.

STEP 4

Finish Cut the Tenons

Use the tenoning jig to cut the tenons as shown at the top left. Once again, flip the parts between cuts to center the tenons. First make the tenons too thick to fit the mortises, then adjust the jig to reduce their thickness for a sliding, but not loose, fit in the mortises. Adjust the blade height so that it just grazes the shoulder cuts.

MAKING THE COPE CUT
Cut back the tenon shoulder on the face of the rails with the table-saw miter-gauge setup to form a cope for the stile sticking to fit over. The cope cut makes room on the rails for the sticking on the stiles.

STEP 5

Shoulder Cut the Front Faces to Fit

Once the tenons fit, you'll notice that the joint does not yet go all the way together, because the sticking on the posts and stiles is in the way. Put your miter-gauge setup back onto the saw, and make the shoulder cuts on the front faces of the rails farther from the end of the tenons than the first shoulder cut, as shown in bottom left. The cut must be farther by the width of the sticking on the stiles.

Curved Open Mortise and Tenon

When joining a curved rail to a stile (as shown in Step 1), use a different order of procedures. First rabbet and mortise all the straight parts as described earlier. Next tenon all rails, including the rails that will be curved, but leave them straight for now. Once they are tenoned, scribe the curve of your arc template onto them, aligning the curve according to your full-scale drawing as covered in chapter two. Cut out the curve on the band saw, staying to the waste side of the line. Attach the curved template to the rail on the backside with small finish nails and flush trim the rail to the template at the router table with a bearing-guided flush-trim bit.

Use a bearing-guided rabbeting bit at the router table to cut the glass rabbet into the curved edge of the rail. Now trim the tenons to fit the mortises using a handsaw and chisels. Finally, make the cope cuts on all rails as described in step five.

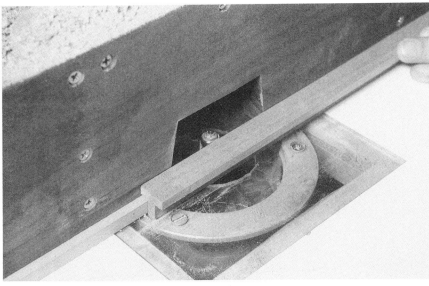

CUTTING RABBETS IN BARS
Attach a support piece to your router-table fence (or table-saw fence) to stabilize the thin bars as the rabbet cut is made.

Making Bars

Making thin internal bars uses a similar procedure, with these variations. Rabbeting the bars is tricky because they are so small that they will tend to rock around while being cut. Stabilize the piece as it is cut by nailing a support piece to your router or table-saw fence on the outfeed side as shown at the top left. Make this piece the same size as the rabbet itself, so that as the piece comes out of the cutter it rests upon the rabbet.

Join the bars to stiles, rails and other bars with stub tenons, as shown at the bottom left. Cut a shallow mortise below the square sticking on adjoining pieces with chisels. The stub tenon itself can be cut at the table saw with the same setup that you use to cut tenon shoulders and copes, as shown at the bottom left.

CUTTING BAR JOINERY
Use the miter-gauge setup to cut both the copes and stub tenons on the ends of the thin bars.

CHAPTER FIVE

SQUARE STICKING— CLOSED MORTISE-AND-TENON JOINERY

The open mortise-and-tenon joints described in previous sections are easy to make and very strong. However, some people prefer not to have the joinery exposed on their work. While exposed joinery shows what it took to build the piece, and can be quite impressive in this respect, it also adds a lot of visual detail to a piece, which can be distracting. For that reason, you may choose to make closed, or *blind*, mortises.

You can still use the tenoning jig described in previous sections to make the tenons for your joints, but you can't use it to make closed mortises. Here we'll take a look at hand and machine techniques for doing so. In the old days closed mortises were cut entirely by hand, chopping with mortising chisels. If you have a drill press or a dowel jig you can spare yourself all that labor and let a motor cut most of the waste out for you, then use a chisel to clean up what's left. Or, get a mortising attachment for your drill press and let the machine make square holes for you.

Joinery Dimensions

First a word about joint dimensions. Traditionally a tenon is made at one-third the thickness of the part it joins. I usually go with a tenon just over that; for instance, a 5/16" tenon for 3/4"-

THE MARKING GAUGE

Use a marking gauge to mark out the location of your closed mortises. You will use these lines to align your chisels when you trim the mortise walls. This step is unnecessary if you use the mortising attachment as shown on page 91.

thick parts. The slightly increased cross section makes a stronger tenon. Beware of cutting the mortise too close to the end of a part, because you risk splitting the short grain between the part end and the mortise. When mortises were cut by hand, they left the part long while the mortise was cut so the chopping wouldn't split the end, then they cut this extra "horn" off afterward. You don't need to worry about this very much when doing machine mortising, but your joints will be stronger if you always leave at least 1/2" between the part end and mortise for cabinet-proportioned frames.

Mark out the Tenons

If you choose to use a drill press or dowel jig to cut the waste, first mark out the tenons on your parts. Marking gauges are designed specifically for this task and make it quite easy. The gauge has movable bars on it with scribing points on the ends of the bars. You set the scribing point a certain distance from the gauge face, and use it to mark the part face as shown.

Bore out Waste

Next use your drill press or dowel jig to bore holes within the scribe marks as shown at the top right. Carefully limit the depth of cut, and don't cut outside the scribe marks. Then use sharp chisels to clear out the remainder of the waste as shown at the bottom right. Use the scribe marks as your guide and carefully square up the mortise walls. Note that if your holes are well centered and the same width as your intended mortise, you can follow the outside edges of the holes as you use the chisel. In this case you can leave just a little bit of the boring marks on the mortise walls, since cutting beyond these means making the mortise larger than you originally intended.

CUTTING MORTISES
Bore out the waste on a drill press or with a dowel jig. Use a bit with a diameter that matches the intended mortise width. Use a fence on the drill press to locate the distance of the holes from the part edge.

HAND TRIMMING MORTISES
Use a broad, sharp chisel to clean up the mortise walls. Follow the edges of the round holes left by the bit to ensure that the walls are consistent.

USING A MORTISING ATTACHMENT

You can obtain a mortising attachment for most drill presses that allows you to cut square holes. First cut the holes at both ends of the mortise, then clear out the middle. In dense woods the chisel will stick if you go too far at once. In this case, take the cut in stages of depth.

Using a Mortising Attachment for the Drill Press

If you want to tool up a bit more, consider a chisel-mortising attachment for your drill press, as shown at the left. This device does the impossible—boring square holes. It has a square chisel with a round bit inside that clears the waste while the chisel cuts the corners. This attachment indeed cuts corners, so you can make a lot of mortises fast with it.

If you buy a mortising attachment, be sure that you tell the supplier the quill size of your drill press. The quill is the round collar above your drill-press chuck which the attachment bolts onto.

Cut the Tenon Faces

Cut the tenon faces on the table-saw tenoning jig as described in previous sections. Adjust the thickness of the tenons to fit the widest mortises, then trim the tighter mortises later by hand to fit. Unlike tenons on open mortises, the tenons cannot be the full width of the part, so you must trim their width. You can easily do so with your miter gauge on the table saw, and a dado set on the arbor. Place the rail on edge, one face against the miter gauge, and raise the dado cutter the height of the new shoulder you need to create. Set the table-saw rip fence to limit the length of cut so that the new shoulder is flush with those along the faces of the rail.

CHAPTER SIX

MITERED STICKING JOINERY

This method allows you to use a molded sticking profile, and presents a hand-tool solution to the problem of joining the sticking at the corners. With a simple chisel jig and a sharp chisel, you miter the sticking itself, but not the rest of the part. By adjusting the exact location of the mitered cut, you can make very tight-fitting, attractive joints. This method requires minimal tooling, but takes more time since you must custom fit each joint. But it can be done with any profile you choose to cut into the sticking.

MITERED STICKING
You can join the sticking at the corners by mitering it with a jig and chisel. This method requires a minimum of tooling and gives an attractive, molded-profile look.

STEP 1

Routing a Profile

Begin by choosing a router bit profile to cut into the edge of your frame parts. Choose any profile you like, such as the quarter round shown at the top right. Cut this profile onto the edge of all your frame parts as shown on page 93 (top left).

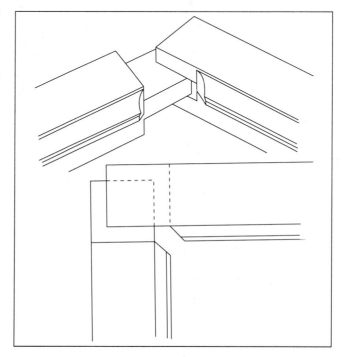

MAKING A BASIC STILE AND RAIL JOINT

CUTTING A PROFILE INTO THE EDGE OF FRAME PARTS AT THE ROUTER TABLE

Cut the Rabbet

Next cut a rabbet below the sticking with a rabbeting bit at the router table as shown at the bottom left. You can also make this rabbet at the table saw with two passes using your regular blade, or with a dado set. However you make it, one thing must be: The depth of the rabbet and the depth of the sticking must be equal.

Cut the Joinery

Cut your joinery for the parts, using whatever technique you choose. A simple and effective joint is an open mortise-and-tenon joint cut with a table-saw tenoning jig, as shown in chapter four. Techniques for cutting closed mortises are shown in chapter five. If you want to use dowels, bore the holes for them before you cut the profile and rabbets.

CUTTING THE RABBET BENEATH THE STICKING PROFILE

FITTING THE RAIL AND STILE
You must trim away a fair amount of excess sticking on the stiles along the area where the rail-end contacts the stile. This is not necessary on the rail-end sticking, which only needs to be mitered.

STEP 4

Trim the Waste

Next trim away the bulk of the waste sticking on the stiles as shown at the top left. You can't easily use the chisel jig until this area is cleared.

STEP 5

Using the Miter Jig

The chisel jig itself is simply a piece of wood with a 45° miter cut into it, and a rabbet which overlaps the rabbet of your workpiece. Clamp the jig and your parts together in a vise, as shown on page 95 (center right), and use the jig as a guide to cut miters on the sticking. First cut the sticking miters too long, try to fit the joint, then shorten the sticking as necessary to make each joint fit. Note that when the tip of the jig points at the tenon shoulder on your rails, or the mortise bottom on the stiles, that the jig is very close to the proper location (this applies only when the inside tenon edge is even with the glass rabbet).

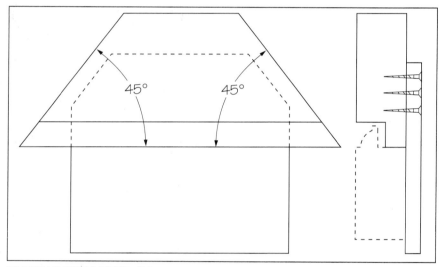

45°   45°

MAKING THE MITER JIG
Make this simple jig out of scrap. Note exactly where things line up.

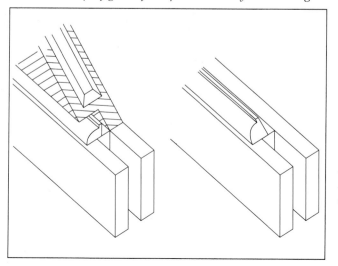

Place the jig on your parts and use it to guide the chisel for a perfect miter cut on the sticking. Note that, for this particular joint, when the front tip of the jig aligns with the end of the mortise, the miter is perfectly aligned.

Making Internal Bars

Make thin internal bars in a similar fashion, with these differences. First, cutting the rabbet on the bars is difficult because the part is so small that it will be unstable as it comes out of the cut. Stabilize it by attaching a support piece to your router table or table-saw fence, as shown at the top right. Make this piece the same dimensions as the rabbet itself, and attach it to the fence with small finish nails.

Second, you must cut small stub tenons and mortises for the bars in the stiles, rails, and other bars that they contact. The finished stub tenon joint is shown on page 92 (top). Make this joint by hand with chisels and a fine-toothed handsaw. Note that you can cut the stub tenons with a table-saw setup similar to the setup in chapter four.

Mitering Curved Rails

Mitering the sticking where a curved rail meets a stile cannot be done using the miter jig, because the cuts must be made at an angle other than 45°. Do these by hand with a cut-and-fit approach. Fit the joint together as close as you can, and make pencil marks on the two stickings approximating the line of cut. Disassemble the parts and cut the joints by hand, but cut them too large at first. Fit them again, and continue trimming until they fit just right.

The support piece in the lower left of this photo contacts the freshly cut rabbet on the thin bar and holds the bar in position as the remainder of the cut is made.

USING THE MITER JIG
The miter jig positions the chisel where it can make an accurate 45° cut on the sticking. Slide the jig back and forth along the part to change the location of the cut and thus the fit of the miter.

ROUTER COPE-AND-STICK JOINERY

Using specialized bits at the router table to produce rabbeted joints for glazed cabinets has several advantages. You get a molded sticking edge that looks good, and the joints fit very tightly at the corners. You can make your parts in a production fashion, eliminating the need to carefully fit each joint as with mitered sticking. But the tradeoff is expense—you'll need to spend between $50 and $100 for a bit set that is designed for one purpose only.

Almost every router-bit manufacturer makes bits that produce a cope-and-stick joint (often called *stile and rail*) for making kitchen-cabinet doors that have a groove for a wood panel. Some of these can be easily adapted so that there is a rabbet below the sticking rather than a groove, so glass can be installed. When you do this, however, the tenon-and-groove joint is eliminated, so you must incorporate other joinery. This is easy to do with open mortises and loose tenons, or dowels if you choose.

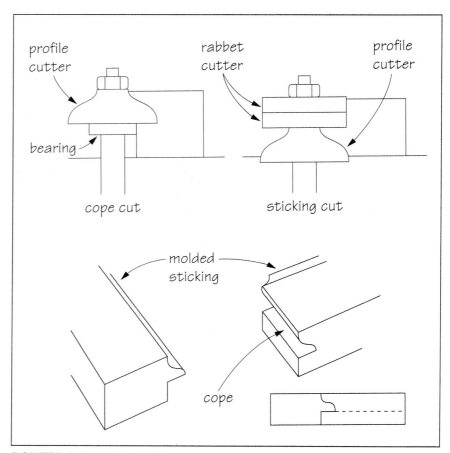

ROUTER AND COPE STICK

Buying Cope-and-Stick Bits

Unless you are doing production cabinetwork, the best type of cope-and-stick router bit set to get is a stacking reversible set such as the one shown at the bottom right. These are among the least expensive of all such sets, are adjustable for the fit between the cope and stick, and

COPE-AND-STICK BITS
This reversible cope-and-stick bit set uses one cutter to make both the sticking and cope profiles. The set has two rabbeting cutters, rather than one, so it can make a glass rabbet rather than a panel groove.

will produce an excellent result with care. Remember that you must get a set that has the additional rabbeting cutter for making a glass rabbet. Several such sets are listed in the supplier list on page 54.

Using a Bit Set

When you get your bit set, make test cuts with it to learn how the set works. Arrange the cutters on the arbor in one way to make the cope cuts, then rearrange them on the arbor as shown in the drawing to make the sticking cuts. Use the shims to adjust the thickness of the sticking so that it fits in the cope snugly with no gaps. Once you are familiar with how the bit set works, use the following procedures to produce joints for straight stiles and rails, curved rails and thin internal bars.

Making Straight Stiles and Rails

The easiest joint to make with your bit set is for straight stiles and rails, such as the joint to the right of the bit set shown at the top right. To make this joint, first cut all the stiles and rails to width and length. Remember that the rail ends contact the bottom of the rabbet on the stiles, fitting over the sticking, so the rails are longer than the distance between stickings on the stiles. Now set up the cope and make cope cuts on the ends of all rails as shown at the center right.

Cut Sticking Profile

Now rearrange the cutters on the bit arbor to cut the sticking profile, as shown at the bottom right. It's best not to make the whole cut in one pass. First adjust your fence so that the cutter only removes about ⅛" of wood, and run all your parts. Then set it to the full width, and run the

MOLDED STICKING WITH A ROUTER
With the router bit set shown, and a tenoning jig for the table saw, you can make glazed frames with molded sticking as shown. The molded sticking is joined at the corners by means of a cope cut on the rail ends which fits over the sticking on the stile (or post). Loose tenons fit into open mortises on both the rails and stiles.

MAKING COPE CUTS ON RAILS
An auxiliary fence clamped on the base router-table fence makes the throat distance smaller and safer. Use a wide backup piece behind your part to stabilize it and reduce tearout where the bit comes through.

MAKING STICKING CUTS ON STILES
In this configuration, the guide bearing is not used, so you must carefully adjust the fence to give you the correct width of cut. Adjust the cutter height to fit the cope location.

parts again. This extra step reduces tear-out on the sticking edge.

Safely Cutting Small Sections

Cut the sticking on very short parts in two stages. Set up the bit with the sticking profile and the guide bearing, and make the cut with the part clamped in a wooden hand screw as shown at the top right. Then set up the bit with the rabbeting cutters and the guide bearing, and cut the rabbet in a similar way.

Your rails will now fit over your stiles, cope matching sticking. But this joint does not have enough glue area for a strong joint. Use a table-saw tenoning jig as shown in chapter four to cut open mortises on both stile and rail, and glue in loose tenons to produce a strong joint. Note that the mortises must be located below the sticking, or when you cut the mortise on the rail you will cut away a visible part of the sticking.

Curved Cope and Stick

Curved rails require a different order of procedures. First do all the procedures on straight parts, except the open mortises, as explained on the previous page. Cut the curved rails to length and rip them to a width greater than the largest width of the finished rail. You will need a curved template for flush trimming the curved edge. See chapter two for making such a template with a router arcing jig. Trace the template's curve onto the rail in its correct location according to the full-scale drawing of your project as explained at the center right. Make the tracing on the backside, which will not be seen.

Cut out the Curve

Cut out the curve on the band saw, staying to the waste side of the line. Attach the template to the rail with

WORKING SAFELY
Very short parts are too difficult to stick and rabbet in one pass. Do them in two steps using the bit with the guide bearing and holding the part in a clamp.

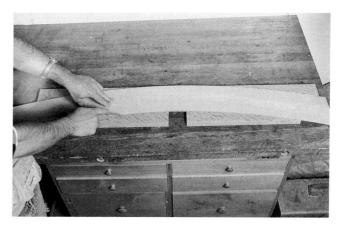

LOCATING THE TEMPLATE
Trace the rail curve onto the part with your template. You must know where to locate the template, and the best way is by making a full-scale drawing that shows where things line up.

FLUSH TRIMMING WITH THE TEMPLATE
Flush trim the curve onto the rail following your template.

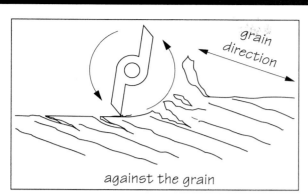

AGAINST

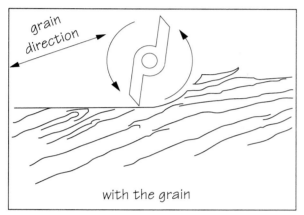

WITH

GRAIN DIRECTION

Grain is a physical reference to the cellular structure of wood, rather than a reference to the aesthetic qualities of wood. Beautiful wood is said to have attractive *figure*. Grain direction refers to the orientation of the wood fibers in relation to the edge of the piece of wood they are in. This is important to the woodworker: When tools are made to cut against the grain, they tend to tear the surface as shown here because the fibers are pulled up by the cutter.

When cutting with the grain, the fibers still break ahead of the cutter, but they break away from the intended surface and toward the waste, where the broken sections will be cut away. Always try to orient parts to be cut in a router or other tool so that the cut will be with the grain, to reduce the likelihood of tearout.

CUTTING STICKING ON CURVED RAILS
Cut the sticking on curved rail edges using the profile cutter and guide bearing as shown.

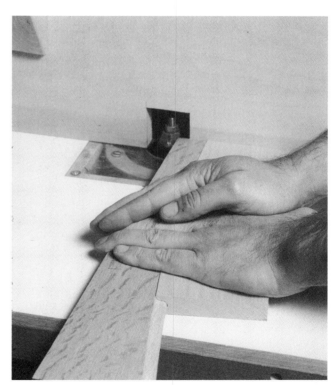

USING THE COPE BLOCK
Use a cope block that fits over the curved sticking to support the rail while you cope its ends. The cope block also prevents tearout on the sticking during the cut. Note that when coping the other side of the rail, all you need is a straight support block on the top edge of the rail.

small finish nails on the backside, lined up with the scribed line. Flush trim the rail to the template, as shown on page 98 (bottom right), at the router table with a bearing-guided flush-trim bit.

Cut Sticking Profile

Remove the template and cut the sticking profile on the curve with your bit set up with the profile cutter and the guide bearing, which will follow along the edge of the curve, as shown on page 99 (top right). Then cut the rabbet below the sticking using the rabbeting cutters and the guide bearing.

Make a cope block that fits the curve of your rail, as shown at the top right and in procedural drawing "Making a Curved Cope Block." Trace the curve of the rabbet onto scrap, and cut out this curve on the band saw. Cut a cope onto this curve by riding on the guide bearing on the bit set. Place the cope block on the rail, and trace the line of the rail end onto the cope block as shown in the drawing. Cut this line on the band saw. Use this cope block to guide the rail through the cope cut, as shown on page 99 (bottom right). Be sure that the cope block fits the sticking closely at the point of cut to reduce tear-out. If it is loose, place masking tape on the sticking at this point so that the sticking wedges into the cope block.

Cope all curved rails in this manner, then cut the open mortises on all rails and stiles.

Making Bars

To make thin internal bars, first cut to length several pieces of wide stock at the lengths you need for your bars. Again—remember to determine these lengths by measuring between rabbets, not between stickings on adjoining stiles, rails and bars. Next,

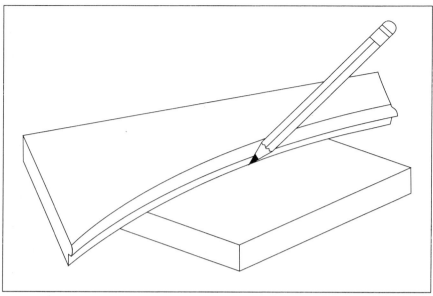

MAKING A CURVED COPE BLOCK

Trace the rabbet curve of your curved rail onto a wide piece of scrap of the same thickness. Cut to the line on a band saw, then smooth the edge with a stationary sander or by hand sanding.

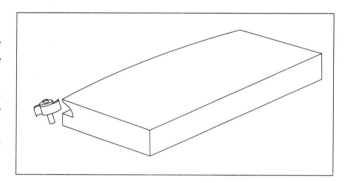

Cut the cope profile into the curved edge of the cope block.

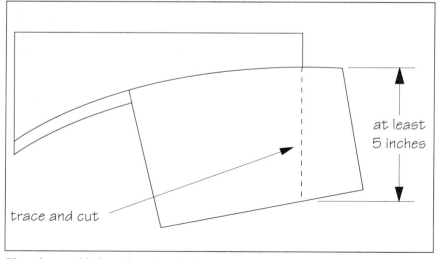

at least 5 inches

trace and cut

Place the cope block on the rail with the cope block's cope cut over the rail's sticking. Trace the line of the rail end onto the cope block. Cut out this line, and again smooth it on a stationary sander or by hand sanding.

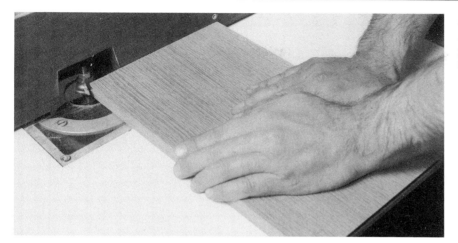

cope the wide pieces as shown above.

Before you break down the cope to set up the sticking cut, make a cope cut on the long edge of a wide piece of scrap that is longer than your longest bar and the same thickness.

Cutting Sticking for Bars

Now set up the bit for sticking, and make this cut on both edges of the wide bar pieces. Use the scrap piece with the cope cut as a holder to rip bars off the wide pieces, as shown at the center right. Drill a hole in the coped edge of the holder, toward the rear, and place a short dowel in this hole to prevent the cut-off bar from being thrown backward. When you rip these, measure carefully to include the face width and sticking width of the bar.

Finishing the Bar

Now take the bar to the router table, still in the holder, and stick the other side of the bar, as shown at the bottom right. The bar is now complete. The joint it makes with its mating part has no joinery other than the cope itself, but this glue joint is strong enough for the purely aesthetic purpose of these bars. Once the glass is in, they won't be going anywhere.

Use a coped support piece to rip thin bars off the wide pieces after sticking one side of the wide bar stock.

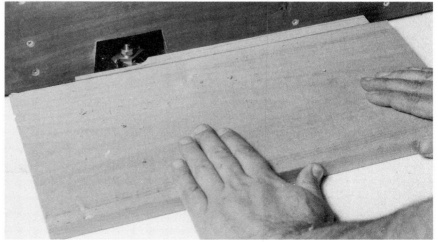

With the bar still in the wide support piece, stick the other side of it at the router table.

Alternative Glazed-Frame Techniques

ROUTER RABBET A SQUARE FRAME

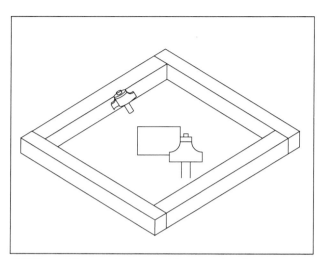

STEP 1 Glue up frames with parts that have a rectangular cross section with no rabbets or sticking. Such frames are very easy to make using any joinery. Next put a profile bit in your router table and cut a profile around the inside of the frame.

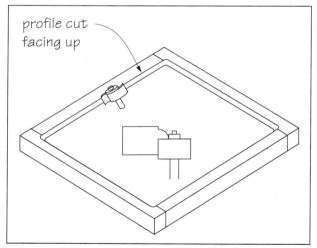

profile cut facing up

STEP 2 Put a rabbeting cutter in the router table, flip the parts over, and cut a rabbet into the edge below the profile cut.

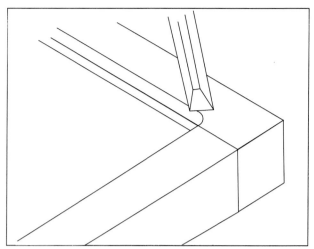

STEP 3 Use a chisel to square up the corners of the rabbet.

Advantages—*This method is fast because the frames are easy to make and the router cuts are quick.*
Disadvantages—*The router profile cut is round at the corners and looks "router made." The joints are not as strong because the rabbet creates an area of short grain on the end of each stile (or post).*

MITERED FRAMES

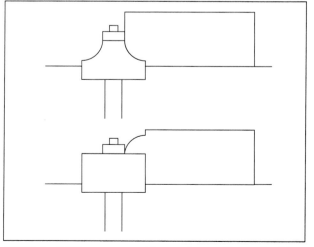

STEP 1 With a router table, make profile and rabbet cuts on the inside edges of your parts.

STEP 2 Cut 45° miters on the ends of all the parts. A sliding cutoff box with 45° fences at the table saw is a good tool for this.

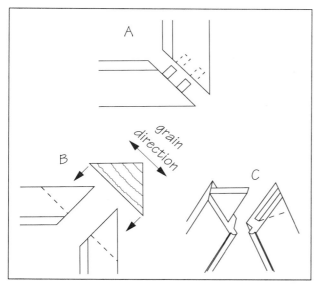

STEP 3 Join the miters with dowels (A) or splines in a slot cut at the table saw with a tenoning jig (B). You can make an integral tenon (C) if you like. This will require a series of very careful cuts either with hand tools or at the table saw.

Advantages—*Mitered frames are fairly fast and have sticking that is neatly mitered in the corners.*

Disadvantages—*All parts must be the same width, or you must make special cuts to join parts of unequal widths with 45° miters. The mitered appearance of the frame is, to my eye at least, less than the highest quality. But this is subjective.*

APPLIED MOLDINGS

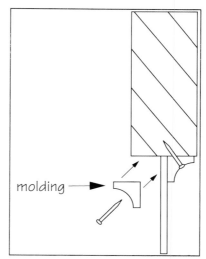

STEP 1 Glue up frames with parts of rectangular cross section, then glue and nail in small molding to create a glass rabbet.

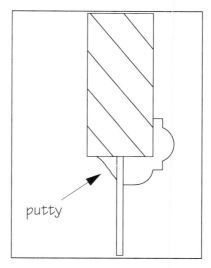

STEP 2 Nail in molding, or use putty, to hold the glass in.

Advantages—*Using applied moldings is fairly easy because the frames are easy to make. The mitered moldings have a neat appearance in the corners. Bolection molding rises above the face of the frame as shown, which gives a unique look that no other technique provides. It's also easy to locate bolection molding accurately.*

Disadvantages—*It's hard to locate nonbolection moldings accurately on the part, and they are so small that nails will split them unless they are predrilled. Bolection molding solves these problems, but you have to like the appearance of it, which is, shall we say, not subdued.*

CHAPTER EIGHT

MAKING AND USING JIGS

Table-Saw Tenoning Jig

This jig is simple to make and gives you a lot of capabilities at the table saw. You can use it to cut open mortises and their tenons, or to cut tenons that will fit closed mortises. In general, you can use it to make any straight cut that must be on the end of a board.

It's not safe to do this by holding the piece upright against your table saw fence; thus, the jig functions to hold the piece for you and guide it accurately through the cut. In order to do so it must do several things. First, it must move parallel to the blade, and this is easily accomplished with a guide bar screwed to the bottom of the jig base that slides along your miter-gauge slot. Second, the jig face must be 90° to the saw table and parallel to the blade. You build these factors into the jig by taking care as you make it.

Jig Adjustment

Finally, you must be able to make minute adjustments of the distance between the blade and the jig face so that you can accurately adjust the location of cuts along the width of your parts. This is critical for getting a snug fit between a mortise and its tenon. This jig uses a T-nut (simply a threaded nut that is made to fit in a hole in wood and take a metal bolt) and a bolt to move the sliding carrier in small increments toward or away from the blade.

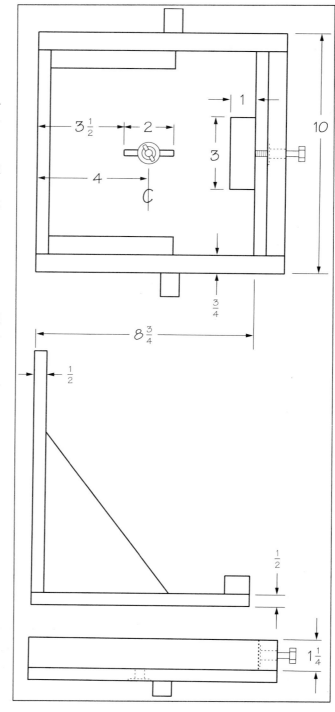

TABLE-SAW TENONING JIG
Screw this jig together from pieces of plywood and solid wood. Take pains to make the vertical face of the jig 90° to the saw table, as well as parallel to the blade on the horizontal plane. Use the adjustment bolt on the right to fine tune the distance of the work from the blade, and lock the two parts of the jig together with the wing nut in the center.

Building the Jig

The photograph below right shows the two components of the jig apart. On the right side is the base, which stays in one place in relation to the blade as it slides in the miter-gauge groove. On the left is the carrier, which can slide to the right or left in the base. Note the hanger bolt that is sticking up in the middle. Hanger bolts have wood threads on one end and bolt threads on the other. It threads into the jig base, and you put a wing nut on the other end to fix the carrier to the base once it's adjusted.

Use toggle clamps to hold your parts to the jig. Not only are they safer, but they provide a sure connection between the part and the jig for accurate cuts. But always be careful not to raise the blade high enough to hit the toggle clamp or the bolts that hold it to the jig. Always attach fences to your jig face as shown for your part edges to butt against; again, it's safer, but also more accurate because the fence helps ensure that the part is vertical.

BASE AND CARRIER
The tenoning jig has two major parts, a base and carrier which are held together with a hanger bolt and wing nut in the center. An adjustment bolt on the base alters the distance of the carrier from the blade.

THE TABLE SAW TENONING JIG
A table-saw tenoning jig holds parts vertically as shown to make cuts on the end for mortises, tenons and the like.

Router Arcing Jig

An easy, accurate way to make curved parts is by flush trimming the parts to a template made with a router arcing jig. But before you even make the template, you must plan your curve, because aligning a curve to straight parts is different from aligning straight parts on 90° angles.

Making Arcs

Make a full-scale drawing of your project, using trammel points to draw the curves, as shown on page 107 (top left). One of the trammel points is a nail driven through the end of a long stick; the other point is a pencil mounted in a sliding piece as shown in the photo. Use this setup to test different radii for your design, and draw the curved parts in place in relation to the other straight parts of your project.

Find the Center

All radii have a center, and you must know where this center is in relation to the rest of your cabinet. If it's a 10' radius, and your cabinet is 4' high, the radius center of a curved top rail will be about 6' below the bottom of the cabinet. Is the center along the centerline of the cabinet, or offset? Determine all this with your full-scale drawing.

Next, see where the curve intersects straight lines. These points show you where to align the curve to your straight parts. (If you are making the case or cabinet shown in chapters two and three, you don't need to do all this, because it's been done for you. Just use the given radii, and align them as shown in those instructions.)

Make the Templates

Having determined your radii, cut out templates with a router arcing jig

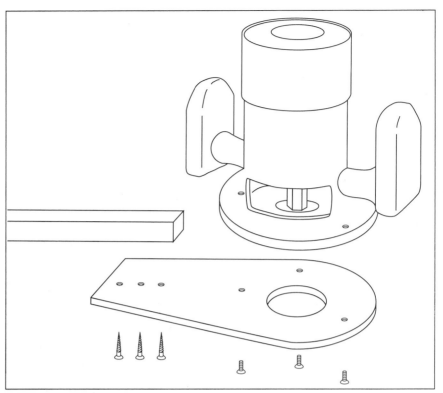

ROUTER ARCING JIG
This jig is simply an auxiliary base for your router. Remove the circular plastic base that comes on the router, and use it as a template to mark the location of the three screw holes onto a piece of plywood. Cut a hole in the center of the screw holes and make the jig long enough to attach a stick to, as shown. Vary the length of that stick according to your needs.

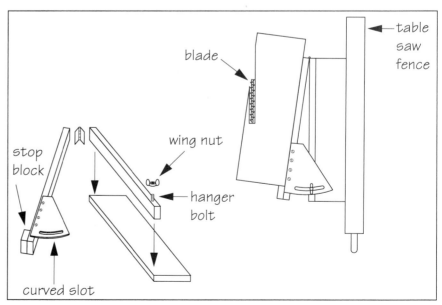

TABLE-SAW TAPERING JIG
Make the curved slot in the triangular plywood plate with your router arcing jig. To find the radius of the arc, measure to the hinge pin. Locate the plate on the bar so both ends of the curved slot are that same radius from the hinge.

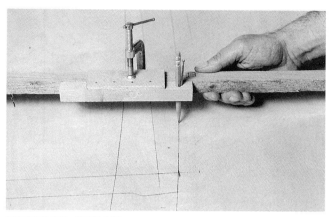

TRAMMEL POINTS
Trammel points are, in effect, a large compass for drawing full-scale arcs. Out of the photo and 13' to the left is a nail driven through the long stick, upon which it pivots. Adjust the distance of the pencil from the pivot by loosening the clamp and sliding the pencil mount along the long stick.

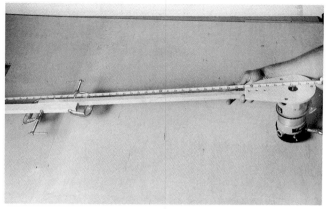

USING THE ARCING JIG
Measure from the pivot point to the outside of the straight-flute bit for inside curves, and to the inside of the bit for outside curves.

as shown at the center right. This jig is like the trammel points, except that it has a router on one end instead of a pencil. Mount your router base onto a piece of plywood as shown, and screw a long stick to that piece of plywood. How long this piece is depends upon what lengths of radii you plan to cut. Clamp another long piece to the first one as shown, and bore a small hole for a tightly fitting screw or nail in the other end of this piece.

THE ROUTER ARC JIG
The router arcing jig pivots like the trammel points, but cuts a slot rather than drawing a line.

Figuring the Radius
You now have what you need to swing the router in an arc, cutting a specific radius. Measure carefully from the pivot nail or screw to the straight-flute router bit as shown at the top right. For an outside curve, such as the top of a top rail, measure to the inside of the router bit (the side toward the pivot nail or screw). For an inside curve, such as the lower edge of a curved top rail, measure to the outside of the bit (away from the pivot).

Using the Jig
The best plywood to use for templates is ¼" Baltic birch, which is

strong and machines well. But it's expensive. You can use just about any plywood, but avoid cheap construction grades because they have large voids that will cause problems.

Secure your plywood template stock to your bench with clamps or nails, and place scrap plywood beneath for the bit to cut into. Drive your pivot nail or screw into a solid base so that it won't move either. As you make the cut, don't let a long pivot bar wobble a lot, because it will make rough spots on the template edge. Sand the finished template to smooth the edge.

Making Tapered Legs
When you cut tapered legs on the jig, a problem arises. First you cut the taper on one side of the leg, but when you try to cut the taper on the opposite side, you must place a tapered surface against the jig. This alters the orientation for the cut on the opposite side. Solution—place the cut-off wedge from the first cut between the tapered face and the jig to realign the part for the next cut.

CHAPTER NINE

MAKING CABRIOLE LEGS

You'll need a band saw and a spoke-shave, as well as patience, to make cabriole legs because it is a time-consuming project. But shaping wood is a joy, and the result is beautiful indeed.

Make a Template

Begin by making a template: Enlarge the pattern in the book, or sketch out your own according to the shape you desire. Remember to leave plenty of room on the inside top faces for rails to join to.

If you don't have solid wood thick enough to make the legs, you can glue pieces together to get the thickness. Match the grain and color as much as you can in this case so the separate layers won't be obvious.

Rough out the Shape on the Band Saw

Trace the leg shape onto two sides of the blanks. It's easiest to cut whatever mortises or slots (for the rails) on the legs before you begin shaping them. With this done, band-saw out one of the two sides, then tape the waste back on so you can see the other set of lines. Band-saw this second set of lines as shown on page 109 (top).

Finish the Leg

Use a drawknife (or spokeshave) to rough-shape the legs, then use a

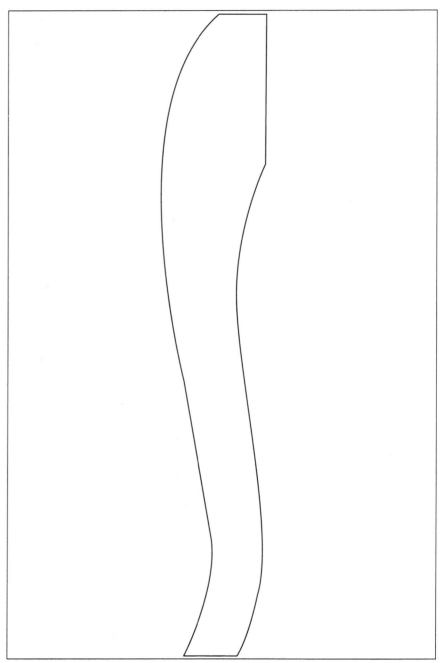

CABRIOLE-LEG TEMPLATE

ROUGH OUT THE LEGS

After cutting out the first side of each leg blank, tape the waste back in place so the lines for the second cut will be visible, and so the blank will be supported underneath as it is cut the second time.

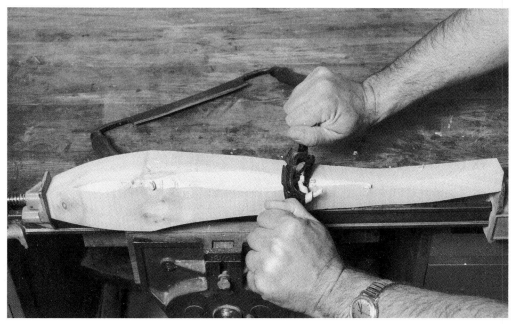

SHAPE THE LEG

A spokeshave is like a hand plane with a very small sole so that it can ride a curved surface. It must be very sharp to work well. A drawknife, on the other hand, is just an exposed knife with no sole, and thus can cut very deeply, removing waste quickly.

spokeshave to get closer (above). A drawknife removes a lot of wood inaccurately; a spokeshave removes less, but more precisely. Follow up the spokeshave with a scraper, or progressive grits of sandpaper. Both scrapers and rough sandpaper remove enough material to shape the wood, so watch carefully as you go.

Compare all four legs regularly as you shape them, so that you get them close to each other. They don't have to be exact duplicates, just close enough to fool the eye.

CHAPTER TEN

GLASS, PUTTY AND MOLDING

Measuring for Glass

Your local window shop will cut glass to size for your cabinets. When you order it, you must give them the exact dimensions of the glass pieces you want. These dimensions must be just a bit smaller than the space into which the glass will fit, or else the glass may hang up within the rabbets and not drop into the bottom. Measure the exact dimensions within the rabbets, subtract $\frac{1}{16}$" from each of these, and give the resulting numbers to the glass dealer.

There are three common glass thicknesses available: $\frac{1}{16}$" (called *single strength*), $\frac{1}{8}$" (*double strength*) and $\frac{1}{4}$" (*plate*). Use $\frac{1}{8}$" because it is stronger and will be less likely to break when hit. Quarter-inch plate is good for shelves in display cases, but the edges must be ground (most glass suppliers offer this service).

Using Glass in Cabinet Doors

The weight of the glass in large cabinet doors can cause the doors to sag so that they bind and will not open freely. You can use the glass as a structural element in this case to hold the door parallel to the frame in which it sits. See sidebar labeled "Glass As a Structural Element" for how to locate shims that cause the glass to push the door up, rather than let it sag.

Cutting Glass Yourself

Perhaps you have some glass around and would like to cut it to size yourself. Glass-cutting tools are cheap and available at hardware stores.

Cutting Curved Patterns

You can have your glass supplier cut your curved pieces for you if you give them a paper template showing the exact size and shape you need. Tape together newspaper to get a piece the right size, and place it on a table. Put your cabinet door on the paper, rabbet down, and trace inside the rabbet with a felt pen.

Installing Glass With Glazing Putty

Finish your cabinet before installing the glass. Secure the glass in the frames with glazier's points, then apply glazing putty to hold the glass permanently. Color the putty to match your finish with universal tinting colors available at most paint stores. Color enough putty to do all the work, since you won't be able to match the color exactly next time.

Roll the putty into rope in your hands, and lay it in the rabbet on the glass. Use a putty knife as shown on page 111 (bottom) to pull the putty flat and straight against the rabbet and the glass. There's a trick to this, but the putty takes months to dry so take your time. Bring the putty to neat miters in the corners. In a few days the putty will skin, but still be pliable, so be careful not to dent it. Clean the glass with a razor and a soapy rag.

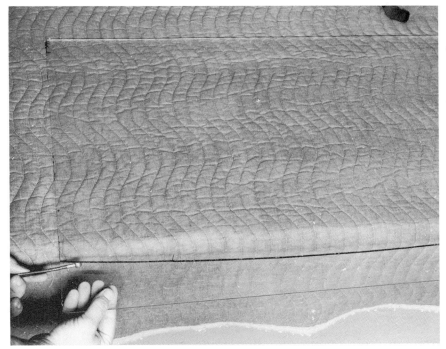

STEP 1

Scribe the Glass

Use the small wheel on the tool to scribe the glass along your intended line. Don't scribe hard, just enough to score the glass—that's all you need. Follow a straightedge to get a very straight line.

CUTTING GLASS

Cut curves into glass (or straight lines) by scoring a line on the glass with your cutting tool, then bending and striking the glass as shown to split the glass along the score.

STEP 2

Split Along the Cut

Place the glass on a table with the waste hanging off, as shown at the top left. With one hand bend the glass slightly, placing strain on the scored line. With the other hand strike the glass lightly with the tool's round ball, as shown in the photo. This will cause the glass to split along the score line, and when it does so, continue to bend the glass and watch the split follow the score to the other end of the glass.

USING PUTTY

Use the putty knife to draw a flat surface across the putty in the rabbet. Place enough putty in the rabbet to begin with so that the knife compresses the putty into the rabbet as it goes.

Installing Glass With Molding

You can also fix the glass in the rabbet with wood moldings that you make yourself. Begin by bringing wide stock to the thickness of your molding. Cut a profile into the edge of the stock with a router bit as shown at the top right, then rip the molding off the wider stock at the table saw using a push stick. Again cut a profile on the fresh edge, and rip off another piece. Finish the molding before you install it.

Make curved molding with the flush-trim template that you used to make the curved rail. Bring your molding stock to thickness, and flush trim to the template. Leave the template on the piece while you cut the router profile into it, then remove the template and cut the molding off the piece on a band or scroll saw, and sand the sawn edge to fit the rabbet.

Use small finish nails to secure the molding to the rabbet, as shown at the bottom right. Predrilling small holes in dense woods will prevent the nails from splitting the thin molding.

MAKING MOLDING

Cut straight molding on the router table with your fence guiding the cut, because the molding material is not thick enough to ride on a router-bit bearing. On curved molding, ride the bearing on the flush-trim template edge while cutting the profile.

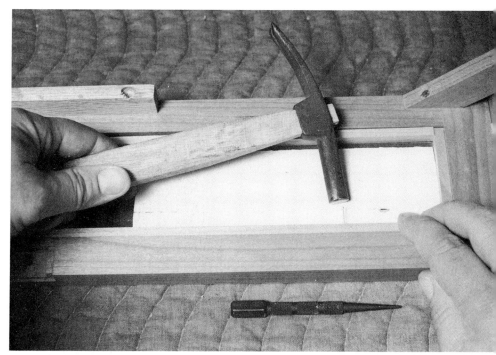

ATTACHING MOLDING

Nail in molding using a small hammer. Put cardboard on the glass to protect it. Set the nail head with a fine nail set, and fill the hole with a wax stick, available at hardware stores.

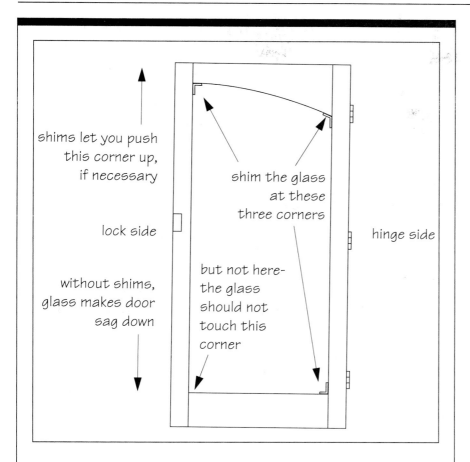

shims let you push
this corner up,
if necessary

lock side

without shims,
glass makes door
sag down

shim the glass
at these
three corners

but not here-
the glass
should not
touch this
corner

hinge side

GLASS AS A STRUCTURAL ELEMENT

By shimming the glass within the rabbets in a door as shown, you can slightly alter the shape of the door so it fits well in the opening. Or you can do this to hold the door's shape so it doesn't sag with the weight of the glass. Don't try to apply more than a few pounds of pressure on the glass with this method.

CHAPTER ELEVEN

INSTALLING HARDWARE

There are two approaches to cutting mortises for hardware: by hand and with a router and template. It takes time to make a template for a router, but once you have it you can quickly cut mortises sized like the template. When you have a lot of mortises to cut, as with hinges, make a template so you don't end up cutting a dozen hinge mortises by hand. But if you only have to cut one mortise, as with a lock, do it by hand so you don't have to make a template for only one mortise.

MARKING OUT HARDWARE MORTISES
The fastest way to mark out a hardware mortise is with the hardware itself. This applies to keyholes and strikeplates as well as locks and hinges.

Lay out the Mortise

Use the lock itself to lay out the mortise for it. Place the lock upside down on the back of the piece it will go on as shown at the top right. Scribe the outline of the outer plate of the lock with a sharp pencil or razor blade. Also mark the outline of the inside box of the lock.

CLEANING OUT WITH A CHISEL
Cut to your lines with a chisel and hammer as shown. Cut too small at first, then make the mortise wider and deeper to fit the hardware.

Rough out the Shape

Use a chisel and hammer to chop on the lines, as shown at the center right. Chop against the grain first, and always be very careful and gentle when chopping with the grain or you will split the wood. Progressively chop and clear waste until the mortise is close to size, try to fit the lock, and then adjust the mortise as necessary. Make the mortise as small and shallow as possible to just fit the lock.

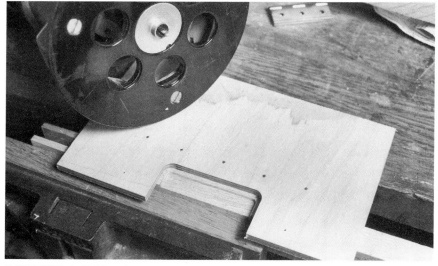

ROUTING A MORTISE
Attach a template to a fence and clamp it to the work before routing the mortise.

Cutting Hinge Mortises With a Router

Make a template for your router and a router-template guide as shown at the bottom left to cut hinge mortises.

The template guide bushing fits the router base and has a protruding ring that surrounds the bit and rubs against the template edges.

The template must be larger than the mortise by the distance between the guide ring and your straight-flute bit. A ½" guide ring coupled with a ¼" bit is ⅛" from the bit. With this combination, your template U-channel must be 2¼" long to make a mortise that is 2" long. This math accounts for ⅛" both at the top and bottom of the mortise.

PANELS INSTEAD OF GLASS

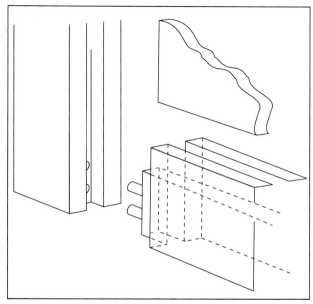

Some cabinets require panels in some frames instead of glass. The joinery involved is similar, and often easier. A panel does not require a rabbet since it is less likely to break and require replacement. Permanently fix a panel into a frame by holding it with a groove cut into the edge of the frame parts.

This drawing shows an unmolded frame with a dowel and stub tenon joint.

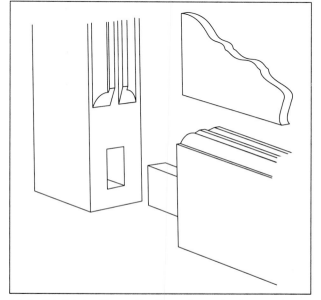

Make this joint with a miter jig as shown in chapter six. Simply make two molded profiles instead of one.

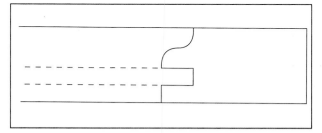

This is the joint that the router cope and stick bits covered in this book were originally developed to make. By using only one rabbeting cutter, instead of two, the bit set will make a groove rather than a rabbet, into which you place a panel. This configuration has a groove and tenon joint which is perhaps not the strongest, but which holds together the kitchen cabinet doors for half of the civilized world. Think about it.

CHAPTER TWELVE

FINISHING

What's the best finish? There is no one best finish; each has advantages and disadvantages, so it's best to make choices that best suit your needs and situation. The three main factors to consider when choosing a finish are the appearance you want, the protection you need, and the means of application you have available.

Oil Finishes

Wipe-on oil finishes give a "natural" look to wood, because they don't build a film of finish on the surface. But wipe-on oil does not protect wood very well against water rings from glasses, or small dings and scratches. It is, however, very easy to apply.

Lacquer

Applying lacquer will build a film on the wood surface which gives a different look than wipe-on oil, and some people prefer this "coated" look. Lacquer protects wood far better than wipe-on oil and dries very quickly, so successive coats can be quickly applied. But on the other hand, you must spray most lacquers (some can be brushed), and few people have spray equipment. Lacquer is ideal for professional shops that need its quick drying time for efficiency.

Varnish

Brush-on oil-based varnish gives a "coated" look like lacquer, and pro-tects the wood even better. It's very tough stuff, and ideal for tabletops that will get hard use. It's easy to apply by brush, but you must wait overnight for it to dry—and the finish will pick up dust as it dries.

But you can deal with the problems that varnish presents, so it is the best choice if you want to build a film finish. Wipe-on oil is the best choice if you want an easy finish and you like the natural look, but be aware that you may have to fix the finish now and again with a light sanding and a fresh coat of oil if water or alcohol get on it.

Preparing the Wood for Finishing

You must make the wood smooth before you apply the finish, and there are several ways to do so. Sanding is one, but it is certainly tedious. A sharp hand plane smoothes a rough surface and removes planer-knife marks in one or two strokes. A hand scraper will do the same.

Taking the time to learn how to use these tools will seriously reduce the amount of sanding you'll need to do.

To make sharpening hand plane irons easier get a honing guide, which holds the iron on your stones at a constant angle for a precise edge. It's tough putting a burr on a scraper by hand, but a proper burr is necessary for the tool to work correctly. Jigs are available that help you put that burr on the edge, and they do indeed make the task easier.

Using Water-Based Finish

If you plan to use a water-based stain and/or finish, wet sand the smooth wood with wet/dry 220 grit paper to raise the grain and level it out. This is only necessary if you plan to use water-based finishes, because only water causes the wood to swell and raise badly.

Staining

Apply stain, if you wish to, after the wood is smooth; do not do any more sanding after the stain is applied, or else you may remove the stain that you just applied. Oil-based stains will cause you the least problems. Water- and lacquer-based stains can redissolve in the top coat finish, smearing and becoming blotchy, but oil-based stains cure in such a way that they cannot be redissolved. You can tell that it's an oil-based stain because the instructions tell you to clean up with mineral spirits (paint thinner). Whatever stain you use, wipe off the excess before the stain dries.

Applying Wipe-on Oil Finishes

Use a rag to apply a wipe-on oil finish, and let it sit on the wood for a few minutes so it can soak in. Use a second dry rag to wipe it off. Two coats are enough with wipe-on oils, since they don't build a film. Once the wood has absorbed what it will absorb, you've done what you can do. Wear gloves to keep the finish off your hands.

Applying Varnish

Because varnish takes a long time to dry, any dust that settles to it in the first few hours will stick. Clean the area in which you plan to brush on the varnish. If possible, work in a dustless room instead of the shop.

Dilute your first coat of varnish about half and half with thinner. This makes the first coat harden well overnight so that you can sand it easily. Always sand between coats with 320 or 400 grit paper to remove dust bumps or other irregularities. This sanding should be fast and light. Wipe the surface off afterward with a clean rag that has just a little thinner in it—not enough to wet the surface, but enough to pick up dust.

There's no need to thin the later coats, unless the instructions tell you to, or unless you simply want it to flow out a bit more easily. But don't thin it much, because you are trying to build a film. Three coats of oil-based varnish is enough to protect the wood and make an attractive finish. Let the last coat dry for a week or so, then rub it out with extra fine steel wool, always following the grain direction. Finally, apply a coat of furniture paste wax and buff with a soft, clean cloth.

INDEX